Nap. Wesley U.M.W. Reading Program
  "mission"   Year 2000

Maj. McIntosh – Eva ✓ did make
                              a different
T H E   Could not
Visitor   Put the
                        Book down.
                        took about 3
Audrey Bueche, Great!   hours to read
                              problem

So good to get this honest ~~view~~
account from a woman's point
of view of being a temporary
president – "visitor" – in so many
different countries. Mary Liz Burris

Wonderful account of a
very special woman. I'd
love ~~to~~ meet her.
          Sue Jeffries

The story of a woman of
great courage and fortitude.
          Gert Osterland

A truly fascinating story and
woman! Sue Bromley

D0920478

Eva de Carvalho Chipenda

T H E
Visitor

An African Woman's Story
of Travel and Discovery

WCC Publications, Geneva

History makes itself in such a way that the final result always arises from conflicts between many individual wills, of which each again has been made what it is by a host of particular conditions of life... What each individual wills is obstructed by everyone else, and what emerges is something that no one willed... [Yet] each contributes to the result and is to this degree involved in it.

Friedrich Engels

Second printing November 1998

Cover design: Edwin Hassink

ISBN 2-8254-1192-2

© 1996 WCC Publications, World Council of Churches, 150 route de Ferney, 1211 Geneva 2, Switzerland

No. 73 in the Risk Book Series

Printed in Switzerland

Table of Contents

Preface

History is too often "his" story rather than "hers". In chronicling the recent history of the struggle in Angola or in writing up the role of African churches in the whole ecumenical scene, no one could ignore the important part played by Jose Chipenda. He was formerly on the staff of the Programme to Combat Racism of the World Council of Churches and is now general secretary of the All Africa Conference of Churches. But what is not so well known is the equally courageous part played by his partner throughout all these commitments, the remarkable woman Eva Chipenda.

I was first introduced to Eva in Geneva as "Jose's wife", but I was soon to discover that here was a woman who in her own right had a great story to tell. Her concern was not only for Angola's liberation, but for women's liberation too. Her passionate commitment to her country, and particularly to the needs of the poorest people in it, the rural women of Angola, shone through all she said and did. I often wondered what sparks had kindled this great enthusiasm and what inspiration drove such energy. As I came to know Eva better, I heard the fascinating story of a life that had begun in a rural village in Angola, but had since spanned the continents. Because she was brought up by a pastor and later married a pastor, the church had always been a home to Eva, but it was a home she had to make in many different continents. Her story is one of travel, adventure and an extraordinary blending of a commitment to home and family with an international outlook and a worldwide programme of activity.

It is a story that needed to be told. It is a story that is thrilling to read. It is a story that will inspire women throughout the world, and may perhaps even persuade more men to recognize how much they owe to those who have stood with them throughout the struggles and who now ask them in this decade to show solidarity with women of the calibre of Eva Chipenda.

Pauline Webb

Dedication and Acknowledgments

This book is dedicated to my family.

When my son Gilbert was a teenager, he once said: "Mommy, you are brave. Write your story."

"Was I brave?", I ask.

Gilbert died in 1993, and his death is what prompted me to write this. Perhaps grief has a way of pushing you on. I think it fair to say that it is grief which has prompted me to speak for the first time.

For years we Angolans have had our stories told. Stories written by people who have never really understood. Stories told by people who have portrayed us as martyrs, savages, heathens, saints or prizes. Never as plain, ordinary human beings.

This is our story. A piece of our existence, an attempt to reappropriate our own history.

I am deeply thankful to many people on whom I could count for help in this work. Here I want to express particular appreciation to some of them.

Pauline Webb agreed without hesitation to write the preface.

Rebecca Garrett gave many hours to this work. I thank her for the time spent in reflection and discussion, for her patience in listening to me and for her willingness to edit these pages. She has made a great contribution to helping me to bring out my sentiments and thoughts more richly.

Hugh McCullum took a great interest in reading the manuscript at an early stage. I appreciate his encouragement and his willingness to suggest that the book might be included in WCC Publications' Risk Book series.

Margaret Odongo took time out of her office work to type pages and pages of the document.

To my daughter Selma, my typist, critic and mentor, I give thanks for being supportive and for helping me to refine my English from the time I began shaping up my thoughts up to the final manuscript.

Thanks to my family as a whole — the people who reared, accompanied and have continued to challenge me. They are the fabric of my life.

I am also grateful to the many people, strangers and friends, who have walked with me on different parts of my journey. They have greatly enriched my life.

Lastly, thanks to God our Creator, for carrying me through.

Eva de Carvalho Chipenda

1. Calomboloca and Mazozo

The Portuguese arrived in Angola in 1482. They came to conquer and convert. The area was rich, and became an ideal place for Europeans to settle and prosper. The first missionaries were Catholics. It was in 1885 that Methodist missionaries from the United States first came to the country.

I was born in the 1930s in Calomboloca, a village not too far from Luanda, the capital of Angola. It was like any other African village not yet touched by modern civilization. The village consisted of at least 350 families, most of them related, and all of the same tribe. Each family made its own houses of mud and thatch: one for sleeping, another for cooking. There were no architects or town planners. The village was arranged organically, according to human relationships, feelings and needs.

In those days, everyone knew each other: parents, grandparents, children, cousins, nephews and nieces. My father's and my uncle's families were among seven or eight families who lived together on a hill. Not far away lived a Portuguese merchant family, who bought maize and cotton from my parents and others. Besides, they made an enormous profit from their shop, where they sold sugar and salt, nails and needles, fabrics — nearly everything.

For the Angolan people, including my parents, farming was their whole life. My mother and father usually woke up at four o'clock in the morning. After saying their prayers, greeting the children and assigning us tasks for the day, they set off on the long walk to the fields.

The only entertainment in Calomboloca was the Protestant church and school. Sunday was the one day of the week that Christians did not worry about going to the fields. Families came from miles around to gather at the church. People went to church not only to worship. They stayed around after the service and talked about their families or whatever else was on their minds. The elders met to discuss problems of the church, usually to do with financial matters, including the pastor's farm and the allocation of duties to community groups and members involved in looking after it. This was a piece of land owned by the church on which crops were grown, some of which went to the pastor to feed his family, with the rest being sold and the proceeds used to supplement the pastor's salary. The pastor was appointed by the church conference, but the responsibility for his livelihood rested solely with the congregation.

Sometimes people would gather for a wedding. At other times there were meetings to discuss violations of the rules of Christian commitment. Protestant churches at that time were very rigid. For example, if a member of the congregation disobeyed any of the ten commandments, especially "you shall not commit adultery", or if someone took an alcoholic drink and was reported to the pastor, or if young people went to parties, the violators' names would be announced at the Sunday service. Until the case had been discussed by the elders and church leaders, the person who had committed the offence would not be allowed to be a member of the church. Later he or she had to repent. This was a fairly regular occurrence. I found it embarrassing to witness this kind of public humiliation, but of course I could not say anything. It was unimaginable for a young person to oppose what the elders said. Their tactics were meant to keep us controlled and disciplined.

The Protestant school provided the daily activity of the children who were lucky enough to attend. Protestant parents were more eager to send their children to school than the non-Christians, the so-called *mundanos* (the "people of the world"). Some parents did not see the point of sending a child to school; others could not afford even the small fee charged.

Although my father never went to school, he taught himself to read and write. In addition to farming, he was also a professional tailor. During the dry season he turned in his hoe for a sewing machine and made clothes for our family and for clients in the village.

My parents were well respected in the village. My father was often asked to solve problems in the community and to act on behalf of the village in negotiations with the Portuguese governor of the district. A very straightforward person, he especially disliked unfulfilled promises: "Don't commit yourself to something you won't do. Better to say no straight away."

My father was a practical man. He told us that although university degrees were important, our ability to use our hands would guarantee our survival. He also told us never to underestimate small actions, because it was often these which had a lasting impact on people's lives.

While my father was often solicited for advice, it was my mother who kept the house running. She was a quiet person whose voice could hardly be heard throughout the day. Although she could not read or write and spoke only her mother tongue, Kimbundu, she knew exactly what she wanted for herself and others. The book of accounts was well stored in her head. She needed no pen or pencil to add and subtract as I do after so many years of schooling.

In addition to the cotton, corn and millet fields that my parents worked together, my father gave my mother a piece of land where she could grow anything she wanted — usually beans or sweet potatoes. He did not interfere except to give her a helping hand. The money from whatever she sold from that field was hers.

We all looked forward to my mother's coming home from the fields at the end of the day. She brought cooked food: roasted corn and baked sweet potatoes. We saw her from a distance and ran to hug her. Her back and shoulders were loaded with firewood and food from the fields. She was happy to be back home and find us well. Her laugh was contagious.

My parents had 12 children, something I discovered only many years later. Only three of us survived into adulthood. All of the others died of various diseases. I was the second-to-the-last child.

One of my first memories is that of a small family gathering when I was about three years old. My oldest brother Julio, who was an ordained minister, and his wife Eva were present. Julio was about 26 years old and had lived away from home since he was 17. Although I was too young to follow the conversation, I soon found out how that meeting was to change my life. The following day my things were packed, and I left my parent's house to follow my brother and his family to a mission station where he was to serve as a minister.

Julio had been ordained as a Methodist pastor at the age of seventeen, after preliminary training at a Bible school. Missionaries needed local people to help them in the implementation of the mission work of preaching and pastoring and teaching primary school. Julio was a bright, promising young man, intelligent and handsome, fluent in both his mother tongue Kimbundu and in Portuguese — the perfect man to be planted among his people and convert them to Christianity. He did well, but the road was rough in many ways.

Aware that Julio was now in the hands of missionaries and probably would live among them, my parents found a new and safe home for me. They feared that if I stayed in the village, I would suffer the same fate as my brothers and sisters, six of whom had died of a disease that could probably be easily prevented today. It killed them without mercy, beginning with fever and headache. Within twenty-four hours, they were gone. We never knew what caused it.

In the early 1930s Angola was still a Portuguese colony, and very few means of transportation were available to us. Those who could afford them bought third-class train tickets. First- and second-class coaches were a luxury out of reach of most of the black population. In a country that had so much potential wealth, we were poor. A long history of colonization had shattered the traditional social structures. The original owners of the land were now reduced to providing cheap labour.

We travelled for more than a week on foot, and the further we were from home, the more we felt as though we were being sent to a deportation camp. When we arrived, we found that the mission station consisted of a single house for the pastor and his family. A second building served as the church and school.

As the first pastor to be sent to this area, Julio worked alone in a region where people had not heard of Christianity and had no particular interest in it. They had never been under the obligation to go to school, and had no use for "civilization". They lived as they always had, off the fruits of the land, eating what nature provided. It was a very simple life-style. Men were mainly hunters, and the women farmed.

In addition to his own family and me, Julio was responsible for other members of the extended family. At that time of large families, those who were fortunate enough to have paid jobs often had to provide food and shelter for other family members. Pressure from the family and the community made it almost impossible to refuse to take on these extra responsibilities: to say no would seem uncaring.

At the mission station, six or seven of us children and Julio and Eva cramped into the single house. By nature my brother was a quiet and hard-working person. Often we all sang together as we sat around the table working in the evenings. Kind to everyone, he saw all our needs and did all he could to provide for us.

At night we children slept on mats on the floor. Julio and Eva were the only ones to have a bed. When one of us "had an accident", as inevitably someone would, several people would get wet, and it was impossible to identify the culprit in the morning. Periodically we would have our scalps and feet checked for lice and other parasites. Lice were removed with a flame-heated needle, and foot parasites were treated by having our feet plunged in disinfectant. Both operations were very painful, and I would have nightmares for weeks. I really admired my sister-in-law's patience with us all.

Totally uprooted, with no news from the outside, no access to doctors, no stores from which to buy even salt, we were cut off from the rest of the world. The missionaries themselves never came to check on our well-being, and became annoyed when my brother insisted on being sent newspapers to read. Getting by on the bare minimum, we were often sick, but the missionaries gave very little support of any kind. Finally, one came to visit; and when he saw the appalling conditions we were living in, he went back and took steps to have Julio assigned to a new post in Mazozo.

On the way to our new home, we stopped in Calomboloca to visit my parents. Although the others only stayed a short while, I was allowed to linger on, and witnessed the death of the only sister I knew and loved, Helena.

Helena was ten years old, and very beautiful. When she smiled she had dimples in her cheeks. One Saturday Helena became ill with fever and headache. On Sunday morning I was taken to church, but before the service ended somebody came to take me home. Helena was gone. I was too small to cry, really. My mother wept like Rachel in the Bible, lamenting the deaths of so many of her children. All I understood was that I had no more sister to play with. I did not want to leave my parents again, nor did they want me to leave. They were good people. They would miss me, and I would miss them. I came to realize this more clearly after I became a young woman, and wished I could have known them much better. But my parents were afraid of what might happen if I stayed, and I had to leave home once again.

And so I went back to live with my brother's family, now in Mazozo. It was here that I started school. Since Angolan ministers were expected to play a dual role, my brother was my first teacher. Classes were held under the baobab tree, with its large outspread branches. We sat on stones that we had found and brought ourselves. We were given a small blackboard and chalk; paper was a luxury.

The villagers in Mazozo spoke Kimbundu, the same mother tongue as in my parents' village, and shared similar traditions. Here, too, farming was the daily activity of the people. Most of the population was middle-aged and old people and very young children. There was nothing in the villages for youth, who had migrated to Luanda.

We walked many miles to fetch drinking water from the river, wash clothes and bathe. Some of us developed callouses on our feet. Sometimes we met wild animals — buffaloes, wild pigs and hyenas — and had to hide or climb trees and wait until they went away.

We were kept so busy with household chores that there was no free time, and we were not even allowed to go to the village to meet other children and make friends. But I had a friend, a middle-aged woman who was one of the members of my brother's church. She was the same age as my mother, and she loved me as though I were her daughter. She of course spoke Kimbundu. Although it was my mother tongue, I could not speak it, and communicated in Portuguese. My friend, however, did not speak Portuguese, so conversation was difficult. Still, I liked her very much. With her I was confident and secure, just as I would feel with my mother.

Julio and Eva did all they could to provide and care for us, yet I was always homesick, and cried so much that I was often taken back to my parents. It was only with them that I felt a true sense of intimacy and belonging. I treasured every minute I spent with them. I was very conscious of their love, of my mother's warmth and my father's respectful presence. They made me feel special and wanted. Knowing I did not like to walk long distances, my father would sometimes carry me back to the farm on his shoulders.

One day my mother took me to the market. On the way home, she noticed a bird was following us, flying above our heads. She cried: "Eva, let us walk quickly. Something is happening at home. The bird is telling us something." When we arrived, my brother had come to visit, and was waiting there for us.

Much of my childhood was spent moving from one place to another. Julio was often transferred by the missionaries, and every time we moved we started a new life all over again. Every year, during the harvest season, I returned to my parents' house. I never went back to Julio's empty handed, usually arriving with a length of fabric for a new dress and gifts of corn meal and smoked fish for the family.

It was a strange time. I belonged neither here nor there. At Julio's I was one of a group. In my parents' village I was a visitor.

This dual life had its positive and negative sides. Very often I felt like an intruder. My parents were still alive. Why should I not live with them, rather than continuing to burden my brother and his wife? But what was there in the village? My home village was a dead village. I had developed new habits and found everything there very monotonous. I could no longer even speak the language. To live with my brother meant the chance of growing in a better environment, an environment that would lead me to better opportunities and advantages for my future, such as a good education. So many times my mind was troubled and confused. To live with my brother, or with my parents? There was no doubt that I belonged to both. But deep in my heart I was a lonely person.

2. Luanda: Life in the City

The big promotion for my brother Julio came when he was transferred to Luanda. The second world war was still raging. I was ten years old and a new chapter of my life was about to begin. It was quite a change to be living in a city. We finally had access to medical care, real schools, stores. We found that city people were better nourished, more educated and very sophisticated. Fresh from "the bush", we looked like *caipiras*, villagers. It was humiliating when people made fun of those who came from the village — "Look at them! They have been brought to Luanda by the tail end of the train!" — it made us feel inferior.

To be in the capital and around the missionaries was to be close to civilization and all that it brings: you walked differently, you talked differently, you saw everything differently. Your meals were balanced. There was running water, electricity, cars, shops. It was a completely different world. You didn't have to go to the fields; instead, you went to school or to work. All this made you think you were superior to the people back in the village.

Living in the city meant learning to be half-black, half-white. The Portuguese colonizers wanted us to become Portuguese: to look like them, to take on the Portuguese life-style. For many urban Angolans especially, this meant living a double life: the Portuguese way and the African way. The African customs of eating with your fingers, sleeping on the floor and dressing in a piece of wrap-around cloth were seen by the Portuguese to mean that you were not yet civilized. Many Angolans, myself included, grew to accept this view, and strove to be accepted as equal to the Portuguese. But it cost money to live the Portuguese life-style: to buy forks and knives, tablecloths, beds. Only certain people could afford these things, and the ones who could not afford them continued to live the African way. However, since it was the Angolan custom for women to eat in the kitchen and for men to eat in the dining room, forks and knives were seen as things to be used in public, formal situations, whereas the women ate with their hands in the private domestic space. So people in the cities would eat with a fork and knife some of the time, and with their fingers other times, depending on the situation.

Black pastors were paid very low salaries in Angola at that time. Fortunately, Julio was able to supplement his pastor's salary with tailoring, teaching and farming. When we arrived in Luanda, he went to work making us clothes and buying us shoes. My first shoes were a pair of sneakers. At first I had trouble walking in them and had to learn. They were made of white sailcloth, and had to be washed every weekend for church on Sunday. I remember the thrill when I later received my first pair of white socks.

We threw ourselves into our new life in Luanda. I finished primary school, started high school, joined the church choir and eventually became a Sunday School teacher.

At the end of the war, when my mother developed severe anaemia and became very ill, there was no other choice but to leave school and go home to help my parents. I took over the household chores: cooking, cleaning, fetching water and wood for fuel, pounding corn, cassava and millet, going to the market for supplies. Having been away from home for so long I no longer mastered my mother tongue, and communication with my mother was not always easy. Sometimes we just looked at each other and laughed.

One day I heard my mother calling me: "Eva, come here, sit very close to me." I did. "We are going to have many, many guests next week. You will have to make sure there will be enough food in the house." She also told me to make sure that her clothes were properly washed, ironed and stowed away in the trunk that served as a closet. "Go down to the village and ask your cousin for help if you need it," she instructed.

"Yes, Mother," I replied.

"Now go to the kitchen and prepare me some eggs." She told me how she wanted them cooked. In utter confusion I misunderstood her instructions, and it took three attempts before she was satisfied. Then she asked for pineapple. I looked everywhere, but it was the end of the season and there was none to be found.

A friend of the family was travelling to Luanda and took a message to Julio, alerting him to my mother's condition and asking him to come. We asked Julio to bring the pineapple that mother had requested. While we waited for his arrival, her health deteriorated. Her voice became weaker and weaker and she could no longer move. The news of her condition went around the village and people gathered at the house. The women were all packed into her bedroom. Mother sang, "My soul and my body I give to you," and asked us to sing along. I sat on her bed. I knew her life was coming to an end. My father was around, but where exactly? He was more quiet than ever before, dead quiet.

When Julio finally arrived with the pineapple that my mother had so much wanted, she could no longer open her eyes. She simply touched him, running her fingers across his face, and said, "My son, now I must go." She left us then. I did not move from my mother's side. I felt paralyzed, empty, vague. Somebody came to me and said: "It is time to leave now, otherwise her spirit will not rest in peace."

I shed no tears. A deep void invaded my whole being. I was lost, lonely: simply lonely.

My mother was buried by a tree not far from the house. Many people came to the funeral. It lasted two weeks, and there was food for all. Some people came and went, but the family was there the whole time. The women cooked and fetched water and the men slaughtered goats, lambs, pigs and chickens to be roasted.

After the funeral, my mother's belongings were sorted and divided up among relatives. I was completely ignored, forgotten. It was as if I did not exist.

About two months later, I returned to Julio's house in Luanda. I was 14 and had missed a full year of school. My father was lonely and disoriented after mother's death. Although initially torn between the desire to see my father and the urge to avoid the emptiness left by my mother's absence, I returned to see him often.

The period that followed is rather blurred in my mind. I could not see or understand things clearly. I felt lost and confused. I was in a state of shock, and could not even cry for my mother's death. One day someone called me a witch because I did not mourn for my mother. I felt terribly lonely, and this incident confirmed my conviction that those around me did not understand my suffering.

Shortly after I arrived back in Luanda, I met a missionary in our compound. He looked at me with an expression of displeasure and said, "Have you come back here again?" More than ever, that made me feel like an intruder — a feeling that I was trying to forget once and for all. Where should I go? I had no mother, no home other than the one that had received me at an early age.

Silently I began facing many problems in school and at home. Mentally and physically I was exhausted and confused. Grief over the loss of my mother was not the only thing weighing me down. Life was hard for all of us at that time. As children, we were expected to work. I was not mistreated; but we were all fighting to survive, and everyone, young and old, had to chip in. We had to wake up very early in the morning to do domestic chores, cleaning and laundry. My hands smelled of smoke from making the fire in the morning for breakfast, and the laundry soap cut my wrists and caused the skin to become dry and harsh. It made me feel ashamed. How many times I tried to hide them after looking at the hands of my female school mates! I also had to walk for about 50 minutes to school with very little breakfast in my stomach, which made things worse. My grades dropped, particularly in mathematics, physics and geography.

While growing up, it was inconceivable to have friends over just to chat. Sitting around killing time was unheard of. I often wished that I had been born a boy. Boys seemed to have so much more freedom, so many more opportunities available to them. I was scared of being stuck in a rut, and wanted to learn a skill and be successful.

The principal noticed the change in my school work and spoke to my brother, but there was nothing he could do. All of us had to do these chores, but some were not as strong as others. I ended up failing my final exams and had to repeat the school year. I felt sorry for my brother because I had wasted his money. The following year Julio encountered serious financial difficulties, and a missionary from Norway volunteered to pay my school fees. This time around I passed my exams.

The next year, Julio was invited by the missionaries to visit some churches in the United States. His wife Eva was left behind with seven children and several other family members to take care of, and only my brother's meagre salary to get by on. In order to help with family expenses I left school once again and went to teach in a primary school. I loved teaching, and it was a good feeling to know that I was actually contributing to the family's expenses. Not a penny of my salary was spent for my own personal needs.

In the home I grew up in, children were not supposed to have money. When we were small, some of us dared to ask uncles or cousins for pennies to buy sweets, peanuts or other small things during the school break, or even ice cream, which was a luxury. The uncles and cousins did not have much to give, but now and then a few coins came our way. If we did not spend them right away, and had the misfortune to let a coin drop on the floor at home, Eva inevitably heard the sound, and that would be the end of it. The money was no longer ours. It belonged to the house. As they grew older, my nephews became very clever. After making sure that there were no holes in their pocket, they would tie the coins into the pocket so that when they walked the coins would not produce any sound.

One day a young missionary invited me and my nephews to go to see a movie for the first time. My sister-in-law gave us permission, and I was so happy. I washed my feet with a stone to make them shiny, and dressed in my best clothes. The film was about the life of Nat King Cole. I remember how impressed I was to see that big handsome black man singing with his beautiful voice. I learned from the movie that he was a pastor's son who had started singing in the church choir. After that we all started dreaming of being Black Americans. My nephews tried to straighten their hair with soap, but they did not know how to do it properly, and it turned light brown — the colour of a child's hair who is suffering from kwashiorkor, a disease caused by severe protein deficiency.

When Julio arrived back from the USA, I was able to return to school again, and I passed my fourth year of high school. In those days there were no universities in Angola, and anyone who attended university — mostly the Portuguese, except for a very few black Angolans who were able to get a scholarship — went abroad. As for me, the idea of going to university was beyond my imagination.

One day a woman from the USA came to visit the Methodist church in Luanda. That Sunday we had our usual string of activities, starting with an early service attended by Portuguese and foreigners, followed by the main service attended by black Angolans, then Sunday school and group activities in the afternoon, before meeting back in the church for closing worship.

During the closing worship, our guest was introduced and she spoke to the congregation. As usual, I sat with the choir. She spoke in English while Julio translated. From time to time our eyes met, and something seemed to develop between us. Perhaps the message exhilarated me, or perhaps it was my admiration of the English language, or the pride I felt at seeing my brother standing next to this foreigner who was speaking a language that he could understand well enough to translate.

After the service, I went outside to play softball with the youth group, and forgot all about the woman. After all she was not the first foreigner to have visited us. The game started; and just as I was getting ready to take my turn to bat, I was called to go home. It took me 45 minutes to get there, and all the way I agonized over what I could have done wrong. Since looking an adult straight in the eyes was a sign of disrespect, I stood behind Julio and waited. He turned, smiling, took my hand, and asked if I remembered our guest.

"You've been offered a scholarship," he announced. "You can choose where you would like to continue your studies."

I could not believe my ears. It seemed like a miracle. I had never applied for a scholarship and to this day it is a mystery to me why she decided to give me one. Later, I learned that this woman was a millionaire, but I was never able to find out anything more about her. I wrote to her numerous times over the years to thank her for what she did for me, but never received a reply.

I was of course elated. I had always dreamed of receiving some sort of training that would allow me to make a difference. My hope was to work with people of different backgrounds and needs so that together we could better our lives. Having observed our people for a long time, I could not understand why we were so poor in such a rich country. I could not understand why the fate of so many women seemed to be to bear child after child, only to have them die in infancy. It was heart-wrenching to watch families being broken up and children sent to relatives in the hope that they would have a better chance of survival, as had been my case. I vowed to have only two children, and to rear them myself. I dreamed of freedom, of extracting myself from the daily routine and overcoming it all.

Growing up in Angola, I felt constrained and inhibited. There was so much fear of public shame and humiliation in the society. According to African tradition, children are controlled by those around them: neighbours, aunts, uncles, sisters, cousins and any other relatives. Adults could do anything to any child — from breast-feeding it to beating it — whether or not it was theirs. No one would object. Children belonged to the whole community, and had no individual rights of their own.

It was no different for teenagers. They were still under the control of the community. Sometimes you would be seen without knowing who was watching you, and suddenly you would discover that you had been reported to your parents or your pastor. So it was best not to say much, not to do much and to walk straight. It was particularly a problem for me as the sister of a pastor, because relatives of church leaders were expected to be examples.

As a young woman, you could not walk alone with a male friend or people would imagine all sorts of things that would jeopardize your reputation. Our mothers were afraid that we might lose our virginity, which would embarrass the entire family. You were expected to be a virgin when you married. Three or four aunts or women friends of the family were given the task of making sure that this was the case, coming the morning after the wedding night to inspect the sheets where the newlyweds had slept for proof of the bride's virginity. Some families even went to the extent of parading the sheets — either to prove the bride's virtue and value, set an example for other young women and ensure the beginning of a successful and stable married life; or to expose the shame and failure, which would signal the beginning of a disastrous marriage and strife among the two families.

There was strong pressure on young women to marry and have children as soon as possible, but with all my ideas and dreams, I was in no rush. I needed time to find a man who would treat me as a human being, not as an object. I had known many women who were beaten by their husbands. They put up with it because being married was their only security, financially and socially. Such a life was not for me. I felt very strongly that I would rather be a poor market woman selling potatoes and tomatoes than to put up with a husband who beat me.

Now I had my chance — a ticket to another world. I began preparing to leave Angola to study Christian education and home economics in Brazil for three years.

3. Brazil: "Go and Learn"

Before leaving for Brazil, I went to visit my father in the village. He was very happy for me, but some of my relatives were worried about whether I would come back the same person or different — as a white person, a non-virgin, or perhaps married to some stranger. Many people who had not been interested in me before were now jealous of my opportunity. My father said: "Why are you worried about her now, when you never have been before? Let her go."

I had to travel by boat to Lisbon to obtain a passport. Angola was still a Portuguese colony, and except for identity cards and birth, marriage and death certificates, all official documents had to be applied for and obtained in Lisbon.

The trip seemed long, although it took only fifteen days. I could not believe that I was out of Angola, out of my parents' and brother's home. I was seasick and uneasy about being the only black passenger on the boat, and so I stayed in my cabin most of the time. Even so I was afraid. I recalled seeing a young black Angolan woman intercepted and abused by two white men as she walked on the street in Luanda. Only with great effort did she manage to get away from them. It was common knowledge that Portuguese men liked black women a lot, but did not respect them. I feared that one of them might come to my room at night when I was alone and try to violate me.

I was met at the port in Lisbon by a man named Mr Silva. He was a short Portuguese man, efficient and friendly, with a soft voice and polite manners. As public relations officer for missionaries en route from Canada and the USA to Angola and Mozambique, he looked after legal matters such as passports and permits. He took me to the student hostel at the Carcavelos seminary, where I would stay for nine days while my passport was being processed.

Lisbon was a beautiful city — the architecture, trams, trains, streets, especially the Avenida da Liberdade, the main downtown area, full of shops and cinemas and fancy restaurants. I spent hours there, sitting on the benches, watching all of the different people: market women selling fish and vegetables and fruit, gypsies reading palms, elegantly dressed women on shopping sprees.

All Angolan school children learned about Portugal in geography class, but I had never imagined it would be like this. When I was shown the Tejo River, I could not believe I was seeing the real thing. In Angola, if we did not know about the Tejo River, our teachers would twist our ears.

One thing that shocked me was to see how many Portuguese women lived such difficult lives. The Portuguese women in Angola were very chic and always stylishly dressed and never touched anything dirty. Angolans were the nannies, the laundrywomen, the cooks, the servants. I had simply assumed that the women in Portugal would be the same or even better off. Now in Lisbon I was seeing Portuguese market women wearing rough and dirty blankets, thick socks and heavy shoes, women with hard hands and blistered lips, carrying huge baskets on their heads, yelling "fresh fish!" Many of them were illiterate, while I was striving to learn to speak the way the Portuguese do. There were of course upper-class Portuguese women in Lisbon, but it was very rare to see them. The women seen every day were the cleaning women. I wondered to myself incredulously, "Are these the people that oppressed us?"

I spent my mornings seeing the sights of Lisbon, and the afternoons and evenings at the seminary, where a number of other Angolan students, some of whom I knew from childhood, others whom I met for the first time, were studying medicine, theology, social sciences, law. It was their first time out of Angola also, and being with them helped to make me feel at home in a strange place.

The academic year had already begun, and to pass the time in the afternoons I helped out in the seminary kitchen or laundry room. The Portuguese staff were amazed because I showed no complexes, either of inferiority or superiority. None of the other Angolan students spent any time in the laundry room or the kitchen — they were too busy with their studies. The staff found it interesting and amusing to have me around. I was interested in their lives — how they lived, their families, the places that they came from. They talked to me about how hard their lives were, how hard they worked and how expensive it was to live. Like many Portuguese, they dreamed of going to Brazil where they believed they could earn much more money and perhaps even become rich.

On my last day at the seminary before sailing to Rio de Janeiro, I cooked an Angolan meal of cassava flour porridge accompanied by stew, fish and cooked vegetables. My sister-in-law would have been amazed. In Angola I had not cooked much, because we had no stove. We had to cook over an open fire, with the pot resting on three stones, and I was afraid of burning my feet and hands. My sister-in-law was convinced that I would never learn to cook.

That evening we all went to the beach. It was a beautiful sight: bright sun on the calm waters of the Atlantic ocean, soft sand and the sound of the waves that took me to an unknown world, a world of my imagination.

* * *

When the immigration official in Rio de Janeiro saw my name in my passport, he smiled and asked, "Eva... so where is Adam?" That was my official welcome to Brazil.

Julio, who had left Angola to do further studies at the seminary and visit churches in Brazil some four months earlier, met me in Rio. We were very happy to see each other, and it was a special time for both of us. We had time to get to know each other and discuss many things that we had never had time to talk about at home. He confided more of his feelings about his life and gave me advice: to study hard, to work towards living independently and to be myself, personally, professionally and in every other way.

The next day we boarded a bus for the 15-hour journey to my final destination, the Methodist Institute at St Amaro, where I would spend the next three years of my life studying.

The Institute, funded by United Methodists from the US and headed by teachers from the US and Brazil, prepared women to do development and social work in both urban and rural settings. From 20 to 25 students, all women, lived and studied there. Each of us had a small plot of land on which we grew vegetables; and part of our work was to encourage people in the villages around to start their own gardens. The only drawback to the Institute was that the diploma it gave was not recognized by the state, only by the churches.

As the Institute's first black African student, I was quite a novelty with my dark complexion, kinky hair and strange accent. The others in turn were a novelty to me: blonde, brown and black people. Brazilians, very much a mixed people, had a good sense of humour and seemed more open than Angolans. They questioned and argued and were curious. At first I was a bit sensitive about their jokes and their teasing me about my accent. But soon I began teasing them back, because their accent was just as strange to me.

I felt very much at home in Brazil. I was free. I became myself. It was as though I had been carrying a heavy load on my back and when I got to Brazil I just dropped it and forgot about it. It was such a different world. The level of understanding — people's statements, minds and attitudes — everything was so clear. In Angola I was blind; in Brazil I began seeing. In Angola I was hesitant and timid, afraid of saying what I felt. My life seemed artificial, trying to be invisible and to avoid problems, fearful of being reported to an adult for what I was or did. It was not that I was doing bad things, but that I was afraid of doing them and being caught or seen. Now, because I did not have to be preoccupied by these inhibitions and fears, I was able to concentrate on my studies and my new life.

One thing I really enjoyed was that the Brazilian young women were as outspoken as the young men. At youth meetings in Angola usually only men would get up and talk. At the youth meetings and seminars I attended in Brazil, I found that the young women also had strong opinions about social, political and educational issues, and did not hesitate to make them known. At first I was astonished, but before long I was joining in with the rest of them. I would even argue sometimes with our Bible teacher, something I would never have thought of doing in Angola.

Many of our discussions centred on colonization and the political system in Angola. I explained about assimilation and enculturation — the whole process of trying to transform us from Africans to Portuguese. At this time in Brazil it was the Portuguese immigrants who were treated as second-class citizens; and it was hard for my fellow students to imagine them as all-powerful colonizers. We also spoke about slavery in Brazil, and they admitted that black people, Angolan slaves, had made a great contribution to Brazil.

I enjoyed my programme of study, particularly working with children in slums and teaching Sunday School. Our supervisor would pay us surprise visits to assess our work. I recall that my turn came on Easter Sunday. All week I had been pondering over how to explain the resurrection to a group of children. In the end, I used an egg, comparing the shell to the cold and lifeless grave, and the egg to the essence of life that could be shared by all. While the illustration was somewhat simplistic, the children understood, and my supervisor was pleased by it.

From time to time, a group of students would go to Sao Paulo to shop or to watch a movie. Sao Paulo was much bigger and more exciting than Luanda, with beautiful shops. On one occasion we sent to see *Exodus*. I had read the book and was looking forward to seeing the movie. Just as we were about to enter the theatre, a policeman stopped me and asked, "How old are you?" Attendance was restricted to those 18 or older, and although I was 21, I was small and looked much younger. Unfortunately, the policeman did not believe me, and I had left my identity card at the school. He refused to let me enter. Two of my school friends felt sorry for me, and the three of us found another movie, *Four Brothers and Four Sisters*, which I enjoyed. But I still regretted not to be able to see *Exodus*.

The school had a strict visitor's code. We received guests once a month, and only on special request. I received just one visitor during my entire three-year stay, my nephew who later got a scholarship from the seminary in Sao Paulo where Julio had studied. On one of his visits, he brought me a letter from one of the students I had met in Portugal. His name was Jose Chipenda. He had been studying theology in Lisbon and finishing university entrance qualifications. At the time I had taken no special notice of him. I assumed that because he was from southern Angola, he was with the Evangelical Lutheran Church of Central Angola. The letter was rather short, enquiring how I was enjoying my time in Brazil and encouraging me to reply, which I did — and promptly forgot all about him. I received very few other letters during my time in Brazil — none from Julio or my family or any of the missionaries.

The three years I spent in Brazil were particularly enriching for me. I discovered not only a new country, but also a new home, new people and a different way of living. Even more important than the diploma at the end of the course were the practical skills and techniques I learned for dealing with the day-to-day situations and problems I would encounter back in Angola, especially the better perspective I gained on the condition of rural women at home.

I realized that sometimes we are what we are not because we have chosen it, but because we are conditioned to be that way. People in villages in Africa have few choices and try to survive with what exists in the village. They do things the way they have always been done, even though it might not be the best way, because they do not see other options. If you do not move from the place you live, how can you see how others live on the other side of the river? Being exposed to other people's lives and experiences gives one a new perspective on one's own situations. It is then possible to say, for example, "We are spending hours every day cutting down trees for firewood and carrying it home. Those people across the river use cow dung for fuel. Why don't we try that?"

Why is it that development in Angola stayed in the cities? Was this the villagers' choice? No. I became convinced that if rural women were given new perspectives on their situations, and if their perceptions were changed, then they themselves would discover different methods of living and developing and improving their situations. There is a saying in Portuguese: "It is not difficult to live. What is difficult is to know how to live." That is what development means. We do not need big development projects; indeed, many Western development projects have been a headache for us. Machinery breaks down and cannot be fixed because there are no parts. Many projects, imposed by others, are inappropriate to begin with.

Knowing how to live is the key to life. For example, rural women spend hours every day carrying water. Why not build a tank and fill it with water that would last a week, rather than going to the river four times a day? If a community gets together and decides to help each other, they can rent a water tank, buy a pump or dig a borehole. People do not need to have these things done *for* them, but they do need to know what it is possible to do.

It was also an eye-opening experience to discover that the lessons the missionaries taught us in Angola were not necessarily applied elsewhere. The missionaries had intended to build a system in which Christians lived separately from non-Christians. They advocated the idea of not mixing with "pagans". Christianity in Angola was based on too many don't's: don't drink, don't dance, don't watch football on Sundays, don't go to the movies. This strict message found fertile soil among the local leaders of the church, for pre-colonial Angolan culture had its own very rigid code of conduct. A son-in-law was not allowed to talk to his mother-in-law face-to-face. A daughter-in-law could not hug her father-in-law, for this would show a lack of respect. In some societies, women could not eat chicken: it was only for the men. During the menstrual period, a wife could not prepare food for her husband. If a woman became a widow, she had to stay in a dark room for a week, dressed in black from head to toe. A woman was not allowed to make any decisions. Boys could not interact with girls before circumcision. It was unheard of for someone to contradict the elders or to speak to them disrespectfully. To go against these rules was to bring disgrace on your self and your family.

With the whole new set of "don'ts" that the missionaries came with, I assumed that everyone in their countries always acted in an exemplary manner and no one went against the Christian code of behaviour. So it was a surprise to visit other countries and discover that not everyone acted in the way the missionaries had advocated. I was unable to distinguish Christians from non-Christians. They looked alike and in many ways behaved alike. All of the things that we were told not to do were a part of their lives, and no one seemed worried about burning in hell. Swimming was seen as an enjoyable sport, movies as harmless entertainment, sipping a drink a normal social activity. None of it was regarded as sin.

It would have been quite different if things had been put in a scientific or healthy way; for instance, that excessive drinking will harm your health. But we had been lied to and threatened with hell to keep us controlled, to keep us obedient, in a cage.

Even before leaving Angola, I had struggled within myself over questions about all the distinctions made between Christians and non-Christians. For instance, we had been told that all non-Christians would go to hell. I had relatives who were animists, but they were good people, and I could see no reason why they should suffer in hell. Many church leaders looked down on traditional marriages. My own parents had been married traditionally before they became Christians; yet they were happy and believed that they were blessed before God in traditional marriage. At the same time, I wondered if some of the Christians I knew did not in fact deserve to go to hell.

In Angola we were encouraged to avoid and look down on non-Christians, as though we were superior. Once again, it was a surprise to find that in other places, people both Christian and non-Christian were equally capable of wonderful and horrible things.

My time in Brazil gave me new insights, inspiration and confidence. I had not forgotten what my father said when I was leaving Angola: "Go and learn. Come back and help your people." I was determined to do as he said, and after receiving my diploma I started preparing for the trip home.

4. Quessua: Life at the Mission

Returning to Angola via Portugal, I found two messages in Carcavelos. One was from my church, asking me to wait for further instructions until the Methodist missionaries decided whether I should go to Norway for training in accounting or return home. The second was a verbal message from Jose Chipenda, the student with whom I had corresponded once in Brazil. He had asked his colleagues and friends in Carcavelos to inform me that he wanted to marry me. Surprised and shocked, I found the whole idea ridiculous! We hardly knew each other, having met only a couple of times and exchanged one letter. I didn't take it seriously.

While I was waiting in Carcavelos, some Angolan students arranged a meeting and asked me to give my impressions of Brazil. When a student asked me to compare the social attitudes of Angolans and Brazilians, I mentioned that the Brazilians were more open and free than the Angolans. Later, another student warned me, "You shouldn't talk like that; you might get into trouble." He was worried about the political implications of what I said, that implying that Angolans were not free would be interpreted as a criticism of the Portuguese government.

Not long afterwards I received instructions to continue on to Angola. I was seasick for the entire ten days. Arriving in Luanda, I found not Julio but my youngest brother Job waiting for me at the harbour. I soon learned the reason why: Julio was no longer in Luanda but had been transferred to Quessua, a Methodist mission station in Malange, 16 hours away by train. I had anticipated staying with my brother's family and beginning my new life in Luanda. With his transfer, my own future plans became very uncertain.

"*Mana*" (sister), Job exclaimed: "You are beautiful!" I had indeed changed. My skin had softened and my now straightened hair had grown. No longer uncertain of my appearance, I was wearing a grey and white dress and black leather high-heeled shoes and carried a matching black leather handbag.

Job took me to the house of Julio's adopted daughter Maravilha, with whom I had grown up in Julio's home. She was now married to one of Julio's former students, and they had two small children. They were very good to me, providing what they could from their meagre financial resources, but I missed Julio and his family. I felt as if something was disintegrating within me, and my initial enthusiasm at returning home began to give way to a sense of loss and the feeling that my future was out of control. I felt more homeless than ever.

However, I received a very warm welcome in church the first Sunday after my arrival. I sang with the choir and played the organ. The youth department had organized a welcome party with a cultural performance for me; and friends and acquaintances crowded around, swamping me with questions.

I spent two months in Luanda waiting to be assigned a job. It seemed that my entire destiny lay in the hands of the missionaries and the Angolan church leaders. The missionaries in Quessua who did not know me had received reports on what I had said at the welcome reception: that many changes had occurred in the church and that the youth seemed to be without leadership. This apparently offended certain persons. Furthermore, some of the missionaries did not know how to interpret my appearance — the joy I took in dressing up. They seemed to fear that this might negatively influence my peers at church. Although these accusations were not made directly, they had serious implications for my employment prospects, and my whole future could be in jeopardy. It was true that I had been invited to a dinner party with my schoolmates. Many elders of the church were also there, but for some reason only my presence was reported to them, although I had not behaved any differently from anyone else there.

In the end, the missionaries decided that I was not a threat and granted me permission to join my brother in Quessua. It was wonderful to be reunited with Julio and his family. Although their house was small, they still had a number of people living with them, and there was room for me. I did not mind. I was eager to find a place of my own to live. But once again, I could not act on my own. The missionaries in Quessua held meetings to discuss where I should live, and a German Methodist doctor found me a room at the hospital nurse's residence.

Once more I felt adrift and uncertain. I had still not received any indication from the church concerning my future. I was aware that going to Brazil had been a wonderful opportunity, and I was full of the desire to be useful to my people. All I needed was to be given the right to serve. But the leadership in our churches seemed not to know how to use the skills of those sent abroad to study. It was hard not to begin thinking that the time I spent away had been wasted.

For a while I did not work. Even though I had been told I would be working at the domestic science training school in Quessua, the director of the school and perhaps some of the Angolan church officials feared that I would have a disruptive influence on the students. They held a number of meetings to discuss what should be done, and finally they decided to let me teach primary school.

Teaching primary school was not what I wanted to do, but I had no other option. There were simply no other possibilities for employment. Because of the way the colonial system was organized, teachers trained in mission schools did not qualify to teach in government schools. It was an unpleasant experience, but I realized that it was their problem, not mine. It was strange to see how people reacted to change. I no longer fitted their mould, and they automatically felt threatened. I knew that wearing high-heeled shoes or polishing my nails or taking care of my appearance did not in any way change my moral values or spiritual standards, but they seemed not to understand this. All I wanted was an opportunity to be useful and to give back a little of what I received.

Teaching primary school was easy: I simply followed the school curriculum. I worked hard to satisfy the students and the school-master. Later, realizing that I was weak in mathematics and geography, I humbly approached another teacher to replace me in those subjects.

The director of the Bible school had also asked me to work with the wives of the students, something I was qualified to do. Since it was a new initiative, we had to develop the course ourselves. We held some meetings to brainstorm on what the women's needs and interests were; and on that basis I developed a programme which was then presented to the director. After listening attentively, he informed me that no extra funds were available to launch the project. The work of the missionaries was funded by their member churches, but since I was not a missionary, no support was possible.

I was stunned, but determined to go through with this project. Since there was no possibility of a grant, I asked for a start-up loan, which the director agreed to give us. The next step was to request classroom space and go to Malange and buy kitchen essentials. We organized courses in cooking, sewing, child care and primary health care.

In the morning I taught primary school, and in the afternoons I worked with the women. During our cooking classes we made cakes and cookies to sell to the students, and soon we had enough money to buy materials for the other classes. Regular home visits were made to encourage expectant mothers to go for medical check-ups. We talked about hygiene and women's health care in class, and our work had immediate effects: women learned how to prevent diseases and to provide better nutrition for their babies. Impressed with our progress, the missionaries eventually changed their attitude towards me.

At that time the United Methodist Church ran two boarding schools in Quessua: one for girls and one for boys. The two were some distance from each other and boys and girls met only on Sunday mornings or when a special activity was planned. Even then, the boys and girls were kept apart and strictly chaperoned.

School regulations were strict, but the boys generally had a little more freedom than the girls. They could, for example, wear shoes to school and to church. Those girls who had shoes were discouraged from wearing them. The general intent was to keep girls looking as simple as possible to make them less attractive to boys. Women's place was to be submissive; and the role of the school was to train young women to be that.

One morning, two foreign missionary nurses asked to speak to me. Immediately I became apprehensive. They were worried about the influence I might have on the girls at the boarding school whom I only met at church on Sundays. It did not take long for them to see that I was not as bad as they had heard; and we soon became friends.

The school instructors, both missionaries and Angolans, seemed convinced that the education of Africans should be limited to skills they could use in the rural areas. The cities were considered the domain of the white population and a few middle-class blacks. It was characteristic of the colonial period that it did not occur to many of the missionaries and Portuguese to prepare or equip black Angolans for work or survival in the city. Salvation for Angolan Christians was to be found in a simple life in the rural areas, away from the corruption of the metropolis. Many of the missionaries felt and acted superior to Angolans and did not socialize with Angolans. Even at church conferences, the missionaries would sit at one table, the Africans at another. The missionaries would be served one kind of food; the Africans another.

There were exceptions; and in the short time I stayed in Quessua, a number of changes did occur. I organized Sunday afternoon activities in which for the first time black children and missionary children participated together. I also led the church choir and Albertina, an African-American missionary, had uniforms made for us. Some of the choir members were my own nephews. One, who was 16 or 17, had a deep voice; and his goal was to sing like Bing Crosby. He was unable to realize his ambition, however. After finishing school he was drafted into the Angolan colonial army and never had the opportunity to pursue a singing career.

Once, I recall, I was at the piano when the hymn "Holy, Holy, Holy" was announced. The congregation was so out of tune that I became totally disoriented, and Margaret Brancel, a missionary music teacher, got up from her seat and joined me to finish the hymn. I appreciated how discreetly she came to my rescue. Margaret was one of the rare missionaries who could interact with Angolans as she would with anyone else. Once when I was wearing a light-blue mohair sweater she really liked, she asked me if she could try it on. It was the first time I had ever heard of a missionary wearing a garment directly from a dark skin. Later, when I was expecting my second child, another missionary, Nancy Taylor, lent me some of her maternity dresses. She too did not discriminate between black and white.

I had been in Quessua about a year when I received a letter from Jose Chipenda, saying that he had not forgotten me and was interested in discussing marriage. My first reply was rather cold: I told him that I was not interested in marrying a pastor since, having been raised by a pastor, I was well aware of the restrictions and obligations a pastor's wife must be willing to accept. I wanted a life with wider scope and the freedom to be myself.

I did, however, agree that we could correspond. A few weeks later, a telegram arrived announcing that he had made plans to visit me in Quessua. When Julio learned of Jose's intentions of marrying me, he said, "I don't know him, but I know his father". Since his father was a good friend of his, Julio assumed that the son was as good as the father and he approved of the idea of the marriage.

I began to worry that, after all this talk of marriage, I might find that I did not like Jose when we would finally meet. I need not have feared: when I saw him, I melted. He was calm and confident, with a deep voice, respectful and gentle. We embraced, and decided that we were made for each other. Jose remained for fifteen hours and met my brother and family for the first time. There was a family meeting to decide when and where the marriage would take place. We decided to marry at Dondi mission, in a town called Bella Vista, where neither of us was too well known.

This chapter of my life taught me a number of lessons. I discovered the importance of facing situations objectively, not with scorn or bitterness. Coming back home meant reckoning with two forces: the black leadership of the Angolan church on one hand, and the missionaries on the other. I had been fortunate that some people understood my situation and my feelings and gave me some responsibility.

5. Lobito: The Pastor's Wife

I travelled to Dondi mission with my brother Julio and my niece Isabel in a truck that carried the belongings of a missionary family newly assigned to the Dondi Theological Seminary.

Since neither Jose nor I was from Dondi, I spent the week before my marriage with a Methodist missionary family on a non-Methodist missionary station. Jose stayed with a missionary doctor and his wife, sent by the American board to work with the Evangelical Church in Dondi. Jose worked with the church, as did his father.

The Norbys, with whom I stayed, were old family friends; and Mr Norby offered to be my best man. Mrs Norby stepped in as my big sister and their two little daughters, dressed in white from tip to toe, were my angels. My niece was also graceful in her white dress. Albertina, the African-American Methodist missionary from Quessua, offered to be a soloist at the wedding, which was led by Rev. McDowell, another African-American missionary.

The wedding was beautiful. The afternoon was pleasantly sunny, with blue skies. I was accustomed to weddings in which the bridegrooms were totally serious and stiff and the brides looked down, sometimes trembling as if they were being taken to a torture chamber. In contrast, I smiled throughout the ceremony. There was plenty to eat and drink, and everything was simple and nice. My brother Julio was proud of the lace and taffeta dress he had designed and stitched for his only sister. When he was asked to speak to the guests, he said: "I give you a daughter; you give me a son." At the end of all this it rained heavily. In Africa, water is a cause for celebration: since rain makes things grow and flourish, it is traditionally interpreted as a blessing.

We spent the first four days of our married life at the home of Dr and Mrs Hastings in Dondi. Dr Hastings, the son of a Jamaican missionary to Angola, invited us to his operating room, where I was amazed by the number of operations, some them very delicate, which he performed every day. After watching a knee being sawed like a piece of wood, the human body stitched like fabric, the uterus taken from someone and placed on the table and an eye removed, I felt faint and had to leave.

After a couple days to visit friends in Elende, we were on our way by train to Lobito, the last stop on the Benguela railway. A crowd of people had come to greet their pastor and his new wife. I was told later that they had expected to see me in my wedding dress. I knew nothing of the place I was being taken to. The only thing I knew for sure was that I was married and was accompanying my husband. From the railway station we took a taxi to the bottom of a hill on the outskirts of the city, from where we had to climb a steep, rocky hill on foot. This was the longer of the two ways of getting to our house, but it was less dangerous than the even-steeper goat path. To this day I wonder how I could have reached the place in a long white wedding dress.

At the house, where Jose had lived for two years, a huge reception had been prepared for us. Women had come and cooked and cleaned before we arrived. Many people came, and there was food for all. At the end of the day a small ceremony was held to welcome formally me into the pastor's house. A few of the women took me aside and said, "This is your home; it's *your* house now. You are responsible for it."

Our home overlooked the entire city of Lobito, which stands between two oceans. The salt reserves sparkled in the sunshine. We could see the slums and the more affluent areas; the shopping centre; the well-cared for Portuguese residential neighbourhoods, with running water and electricity and gardens vivid with all sorts of plants and flowers.

The house itself was small, old and not professionally designed. It was made of mud blocks, and the walls were coated with a thin layer of cement. Jose had tried to make it look new before our marriage. His father had founded the churches in Lobito and Benguela, and Jose had grown up here and was well known in the area. His parents had since moved to the countryside, and Jose, as their oldest son, had been appointed to continue the work. The teacher of the church school lived in a similar house on the same compound together with his nephew. Next to the pastor's house, there was a single small tree whose bark was worn thin because the goats rubbed their backs against it.

The area was dry, without running water or electricity. Jose had tried to build a reservoir equipped with a manual pump, but the pump did not hold up very long because of all the animals. Down in the *sanzala*, or slums, there was a public water supply with a single tap for the use of about 2000 inhabitants, and one had to arrive early in the morning to avoid a long queue. The water was collected in barrels or buckets by women and children down below, and pulled up to the top of the hill by two men. Two barrels of water a day were a luxury for us. We used this ration to cook, to wash, to clean and to drink. The water tasted and smelled of wine, because the barrels we used had originally contained wine exported from Portugal. Most days, we did not have water till nine o'clock in the morning. Jose's two young brothers who were living with us often had to forgo breakfast and run down the hill to wash, in order to get to school in time.

Despite the water problem, I was determined to start a garden. The water used to wash ourselves and the dishes was thrown onto the garden. In about three months lettuce, carrots and tomatoes began to appear. Then one morning we woke up to find that the vegetable garden had been harvested by the goats during the night. This happened twice, and each time I cried tears of disappointment and frustration.

There were flies throughout the day and mosquitoes at night. Only the torrential rains could make the entire compound green and beautiful, and then we had to reckon with the slippery mud, which made it very difficult to walk up and down the path on the hill. A lot of mud ended up inside the house, just as the dust did during the dry season, making it a continuous struggle to keep the house clean.

My husband served two congregations. The white congregation worshipped in one of the most modern churches of the city, made of bricks, beautifully designed and built. The black congregation worshipped in a more modest building, crudely conceived and made of mud blocks, which was also used as a school during the weekdays. What made it look like a church was the pulpit and the cross on the wall. It was truly the church of the poor, built in the poorest community of Lobito.

We subsisted primarily on the gifts of the white congregation. It was a real struggle for the black congregation to cover the operating costs of the church and their share of the pastor's salary. Our wedding present from the white congregation was a complete set of household furnishings, including a small kerosene refrigerator, a real luxury for a young couple.

Just before our wedding, Jose had built a small bathroom next to our bedroom. It was equipped with a shower and a pit latrine with an outside door, which was soon reduced to shreds by the goats who rubbed their horns on it.

The built-in stove in the kitchen worked fairly well, though it consumed a lot of wood, and because of a defect in the chimney thick smoke invariably filled the kitchen, blackening the walls even if the door and window on the outside wall were opened to direct the smoke out. There were no shelves, simply a small armoire, which could be opened only if one held on to the whole structure, lest it topple onto one's feet.

The second room of the house had a separate entrance, accessible by crossing an outside courtyard. The room was small, perhaps a little larger than our bedroom, and accommodated a twin bed and my small organ. One day I had just settled down to start practising when I heard something move inside. I screamed; and when Jose and his brothers came running to see what was wrong, they found a snake hiding inside the organ. Although they tried hard to kill the animal without damaging the organ, it was destroyed.

Snakes, most of them poisonous, were a constant threat. The stones outside the house provided them year round with a cool shelter from which they could easily enter our living area. Several times I tried unsuccessfully to scare away a cat I found in the house, until one day I discovered it wrestling with a snake that had tried to enter the dining room. During the ninth month of my first pregnancy, I was in the kitchen preparing a meal when I reached into a wooden box to get some firewood. Just then I noticed something move, and a snake slid out. To this day I have no idea how I did it, but in a split second I managed to wriggle myself out through the narrow kitchen window.

Despite such hardships, I was very grateful to have a place we could call home. I decorated the house with potted plants, and Jose built a veranda to provide us with some relief from the sun. With the vegetable garden and our chickens, the whole atmosphere of the compound was changed.

The work of the church was going well, and Jose reorganized the financial management of both the church and school. To supplement our income I baked cookies and sent them to the market to be sold. Jose's attempt at commerce was not so successful. His idea was to buy oranges and tangerines wholesale from a local farmer and then re-sell them at retail prices. But in the hot weather the fruit ripened too quickly and went rotten. Although we were disappointed, we were also relieved at not having to find markets and take the risk of losing more money.

In the midst of all this, the political climate in Angola was changing. The liberation movement had taken root, and Angolans were openly protesting against the Portuguese regime. Some members of our church had been imprisoned, and it was believed that Jose's life was at risk. Although he had done nothing illegal, Protestant leaders were suspected at that time of being engineers of the revolution, due to their influence over the people. One Sunday when I left the church in the middle of the service to comfort our baby daughter Selma, who was crying, I spotted a man outside with his ear up against the window of the church. The man was a stranger to our community, and I realized he must be a secret police agent trying to catch what was being said during the sermon. The Portuguese authorities were suspicious that pastors were preaching sermons designed to incite their congregations.

So when word came that Jose had been selected to go to the United States on a one-year scholarship, we welcomed the idea. The messages we began receiving concerning the family, however, worried us. The mission board proposed that our infant daughter be left behind with her grandparents. Later, when it became known that I was two months pregnant with our second child, the mission decided that Jose should leave alone, since they did not have the funds to support a growing family in the United States.

The second pregnancy was a surprise to both of us. We had planned to have a second child three years after the first. It was obvious that the child and I would have to remain behind. Did I really have any choice? It was a difficult verdict to accept, but given our options, I preferred a temporary separation to the thought of being responsible for putting Jose's life at risk.

6. Dondi: Waiting to Leave

With Jose on his way to the USA, via Lisbon, I was alone with one small baby, another on the way, and Jose's two young brothers, whom we were looking after until they finished their schooling. Since we had no house of our own, Jose's parents decided that I should come and stay with them at their home in Dondi. Selma and I left for Dondi, with the two boys to follow later.

Although the church had committed itself to ensuring our financial support during his absence, when the stipend for the second month arrived, it included a letter from the church treasurer stating that this would be the last payment, since the church could not afford to finance both an absentee pastor and his replacement. I did not argue, knowing that the members of this church of the poor already had to sacrifice a good deal to pay the salary of even one pastor.

I knew that I was capable of working to support myself and the children, but I also knew that it was unheard of for a pastor's wife to work outside of the church. However, Mary Crosby, a Canadian missionary who worked in the same office as my father-in-law, soon became my friend and confidante; and when I related my problems to her, she approached Pinto Ribeiro, director of the theological seminary in Dondi. Not long after that I was asked to work with the wives of students at the seminary. The work was challenging, and I earned enough to support myself and the children and to contribute to the upkeep of my in-laws' house.

Meanwhile, the political situation in the country continued to degenerate. A revolt started in Luanda, and then spread to other regions. A group of freedom fighters stormed the political prison in Luanda and freed some of the prisoners. This marked the beginning of the war for Angolan independence. The release infuriated the Portuguese authorities, who took strong measures to suppress the revolt. But it was too late. The winds of independence were blowing throughout the land, and young people carried the seeds of revolution from Luanda to cities such as Malange, Benguela and Lobito.

Because of their social position and education, a number of Protestant pastors and church members were under suspicion by the Portuguese authorities, and many church people were being imprisoned, tortured, deported and killed. Confusion, tension, fear and false accusations reigned in the country.

We heard that Jose had been black-listed by the Portuguese secret police. Two members of our church had already been picked up and detained indefinitely without charges, and it became questionable whether Jose should return to Angola.

The Portuguese were fearful. As more and more people became involved, more and more Angolans from all parts of the country were being arrested, mistreated, sent out of the country or executed. One result of this repression was to bring Angolans of different ethnic and socio-political backgrounds together, creating new affinities.

Rumour had it that the Dondi mission was going to be bombarded. Dondi was vulnerable because of its reputation and because of its successes in education and health. The biggest Protestant mission in Angola, it had a large high school for boys, a domestic school for girls, a good-sized hospital, primary schools and a theological seminary. The presence there of many missionaries from Canada and the US aroused suspicion among the authorities, who believed that the foreign Protestants were influencing Angolans to rebel against the colonial regime. Furthermore, the revolution had started among intellectuals, and the colonial authorities distrusted blacks who had been educated in Protestant mission schools. We began to fear for our lives.

My brother-in-law Duarte was living in Dondi, training to be a photographer. He had access to a darkroom, where we decided we would hide in case Dondi should be bombed. Fortunately, nothing happened.

In the Dondi mission there was an old Ovimbundu woman, Auntie Lydia, whom I loved immensely. The caretaker of the girl's domestic school, she was like a mother to the students. She spoke no Portuguese or English, but despite our inability to communicate verbally, she visited me often. I felt that she was the only Angolan at the mission who truly cared for and loved me and the babies, and her presence was a joy. It was her sincerity that drew me to her.

Strangely enough, I found more warmth and companionship at Dondi among the missionaries than among my own people, perhaps because I was also considered a foreigner by the local Angolans. I could neither speak nor understand Umbundu, the local language; but when the missionaries discovered this, they did not make me feel as much like an outsider as the local people did. Some of the local people even asked me, "Why don't you speak Umbundu?", though it did not seem to occur to them to wonder why they could not speak my language.

In any case, I had other priorities in mind: to get out of the country. The babies and I spent a month in Silva Porto, a small town in the province of Bie, in the south of Angola, with a Portuguese couple who were members of our Portuguese congregation in Lobito. A friendship had grown between us over the years, and I looked forward to seeing them again. We travelled to Silva Porto by train, and the month there was a wonderful change from the turmoil.

When we returned to Dondi, we found many of the expatriates making arrangements to have their families sent home. Students at the seminary were becoming restless and the situation was volatile. My father-in-law, sensing my distress, approached one of the missionaries, and was sent to Luanda to make arrangements for me and the children to leave for Portugal. After an anxious wait, approval came, and we began to make preparations.

We were driven to Nova Lisboa (now Huambo) and spent the night in a missionary home. The next day we flew by helicopter to Luanda, where we were met by my nephew Joao, who took me to his home until the day of our departure. I was unable to meet with Julio who was in Quessua or my father in my home village, neither of whom had seen my children. My nephews took us to the airport, and we parted.

It was my first long airplane trip, and we were the only black passengers. Naturally, I was nervous. Our first stop was in Lagos, where we were asked to disembark. I was amazed by what I saw. There were many Nigerian women dressed very differently from Angolans. They looked more "African" to me in their long skirts, head scarves in many different styles, dresses made of brightly coloured fabrics with many different patterns. Urban Angolan women usually dressed in European clothes and fabrics. In the rural areas, each ethnic group had its own style of dressing, but they were generally much less flamboyant than the Nigerians.

Being somewhat isolated from what was happening politically in other African countries, I was shocked to see many white men in army uniforms with guns. I suppose the British army was protecting the airport from invasion by Nigerian freedom fighters, but since I knew no English, I could not find out what was going on.

At one point I was tempted to hide in the toilets, miss the plane, obtain political asylum, and then try to join Jose. But what about our suitcase, I wondered, and how would I make myself understood? So when our flight's departure was announced, I took my eight-month old baby in my arms, clutched two-and-a-half-year-old Selma's hand, and we boarded.

7. Escaping from Portugal

In Lisbon we were greeted by the same Mr Silva who met me the first time I passed through Portugal on my way to study in Brazil. He took us to a student hostel.

"How was the temperature in Angola when you left?", he asked. "Oh, not so bad," I replied. "Almost the beginning of the cold season."

But I had misunderstood him. "Oh, I don't want to know about the weather," he responded. "I was wondering what the *political* temperature is like."

Before leaving Angola I had been warned to be cautious of any questions regarding politics, whether they were asked by Portuguese or Africans. Unfortunately, both races were used as informers.

"There is nothing happening in the cities, but there is insecurity in the rural areas," I said.

"You came at the wrong time," Mr Silva said. "Many Angolans and Mozambican students have fled the country." I did not like this news at all and began to worry if I would ever make it to the USA.

I did not begin to search for a way of joining Jose right away, because I did not know how to go about obtaining a passport without arousing attention. The situation in Portugal was very tense. Portuguese soldiers had been sent to Angola to fight, and their families and friends were worried, not knowing if they would come back alive. It was a vicious war, and no one knew how long it would last.

The day before I left Angola, the media had announced that Jose's brother Daniel had been imprisoned in Portugal, where he had gone several years earlier as a professional football player. When Angolan students started escaping from Portugal, Daniel was suspected of being involved. I realized that I had to be cautious in my movements because any black person in Portugal during this time was under suspicion and could be accused of anything. Simply knowing about how friends had escaped could be perceived as treason. Among the Angolan and Mozambican students to flee the country was my younger brother Job, who had left before our arrival because he was afraid of being arrested or harassed.

On my second day at the student hostel, I met a young Angolan woman named Mimosa. We had gone to school together, and our families knew each other well.

"What are you doing here?", I asked. "Are you nearly finished your studies?"

"Don't you know?", she said in a low voice. "Most of us have already left the country. I am in the last group that is leaving today in a few hours. I've just come here today to collect a few of my belongings."

She searched for something in her bag and gave me a piece of paper with a name on it, saying: "Keep this name carefully. You may need it some day." She left, and I never saw her again.

I began to panic. Not knowing what to do or where to begin, I concentrated on looking after my babies and keeping us all safe and healthy. Five months later, I still had not accomplished anything. One day in the spring of 1961, a US missionary whom I had known at Dondi arrived at the hostel and asked to see me. He had been home on leave, and now on his way back to Angola stopped to see how I was getting along.

It was nice to see a familiar face, and I appreciated his concern for me. He questioned me curiously and then told me that Mr Silva should be able to help me with the passport application.

I met with Mr Silva, filled out many forms and signed many documents. There always seemed to be something wrong with them. Either my signature was not clear, or I had used black ink rather than blue, or I had used a ball point rather than a fountain pen. I began to doubt Mr Silva's sincerity.

One cold and foggy morning I was summoned by the secret police. I took Selma along. The taxi driver dropped us at the building and directed us to go upstairs, where we were made to wait in a cold room for nearly an hour before being called into the office. Two well-dressed men in their thirties asked a series of questions: "Where are the other Angolan students?", "What is your political affiliation?", "Where is your husband?" "Who sent him there?" My mind was in a spin, particularly when they both questioned me at the same time. Fortunately, I knew very little, so that even if I had wanted I could not give them any information. Selma, totally unaware of the gravity of the situation, provided distraction by chatting with my interrogators and asking questions about the pictures hanging on the walls of the office.

Finally the interview was ended, and we returned to the hostel. I was relieved that the ordeal was over, but the outcome was inconclusive. I had gone to the interview hoping that a passport would be granted and that I would be given clearance to join Jose in the United States. The request was neither granted nor denied, and I was no further ahead than I had been.

Two weeks later, I was again summoned by the secret police. This time I went alone. Again, I was made to wait in a cold room before being called in. Two men I had never seen before told me: "You have been called in so that we could inform you that you have *not* been granted permission to leave Portugal for the USA. You may stay in Portugal or return to Angola, but your movements will be watched. We want your husband."

"Over my dead body," I promised myself. I left the secret police and went straight back to the hostel. Suddenly I felt light, free as a bird. The situation was finally clear. I had tried to abide by the law, but the law-makers were not on our side. They abused their authority and enjoyed making others suffer. Fear and bribes were used to turn people against their own families.

Suspecting that Mr Silva was working for the secret police, I decided to find my own way out. Some Canadian and British women missionaries were staying at the hostel, and we had become friends. They had been sent to Portugal to learn the language, but they decided to go back home after being suspected of helping students escape from Portugal. One of them called me into her room as she was packing and gave me the name of a contact person whom I will call "the Boss", and told me that she had already informed him of my situation. She advised me to try to reach him only if the situation became desperate; otherwise he would contact me. The name on the piece of paper was the same one Mimosa had given me the day she left. I realized that this was my only hope.

Jose and I had kept our correspondence to a minimum to protect the family. But I did write to tell him of our difficulties and said I would like to enroll in a dressmaking class to keep myself occupied. Funds were wired from the USA, and I started taking lessons. It was good to have a reason to spend some time away from the hostel. A white South African family who had come to stay at the hostel generously offered to look after the children during my classes. They were very kind and we spent time together talking and playing table tennis. Having heard only negative reports about how whites in South Africa treated black people, I was surprised to find that they were very nice people. Then, for reasons I never learned, the family was asked to leave the country about three months after their arrival. Their departure left me desolate.

Finally "the Boss" called. Arrangements were made for me to meet his wife at a particular spot in an amusement park. As I was scanning the crowd for a woman of the description he had given me, she walked straight over to me and asked if my name was Eva Chipenda. Clearly it was easy for her to spot me, since I was the only black person in the park.

Communication between us was difficult because she spoke Spanish and I spoke Portuguese, but we managed to get along. At the second meeting I met her husband, a tall, bald man with friendly blue eyes. I trusted him immediately, and he expressed his willingness to help us, in spite of the difficulty of smuggling out two small children. He told me to be cautious, because the secret police were well organized and had infiltrated the Angolan community in Portugal. It was even possible that some of my own compatriots and friends could be informants. I took his warning seriously.

During this time, I learned of the imprisonment of my father, my brother Julio, and three of his sons in Angola. The news made my blood boil. Many Angolans who had no direct involvement in the liberation war were being arrested and tortured. This was a tactic the Portuguese used to collect information about the guerilla movement and its supporters. Under the circumstances, even a normally innocent action like offering food to someone could be construed as subversive by the authorities.

One day on my way back from design class, two *quintadeiras* (women street vendors) boarded the tram I was riding. Since I was the only black passenger, they immediately assumed I was Angolan and began to spew their hatred at me. Angola was the first Portuguese colony to start a war for independence, and many Portuguese women were angry and bitter that their sons were dying in Angola. Obviously it did not occur to these women on the tram that I was not responsible for their presence in Angola in the first place, nor had they ever considered the Angolan people's suffering, both past and present. The Portuguese people in general were ignorant of what went on in its colonies. Frightened, I sat silently and as still as possible until, to my great relief, the tram stopped and the vendors got out with their vegetable baskets.

One day it became obvious that I was being followed. Every time I went out, particularly to my design classes, I saw the same man walking either beside or behind me. I could not tell if it was the police or someone sent by "the Boss". The atmosphere of fear that permeated all aspects of daily life made me very cautious. "The Boss" and I met several times for briefings. The plans were going ahead, and I wrote a letter to Jose informing him of our preparations. I asked an acquaintance of Jose's, who was staying at the hostel on his way to Latin America, to mail the letter once he was outside of Portugal, given the sensitivity and danger of the situation.

My brother Julio and my father were excellent tailors, and during my childhood I had spent many hours watching

Julio take measurements, lay out and cut fabric, and then piece garments together. Thanks to that experience, I earned my diploma with honours. Meanwhile, the situation in Angola was continuing to deteriorate. One day word reached me that a relative of mine was among a group of Angolan political prisoners who had been sent to a deportation camp in the Cape Verde Islands. I quickly prepared a basket of essentials like soap and toothpaste, and sent it to them.

Often I felt very lonely and powerless; at other times, I raged at the whole situation, realizing that all this could have been avoided if only we could learn to follow the Golden Rule. Then one Saturday morning I received a telephone call. "Are you Mrs Chipenda?", the voice asked.

"Yes," I answered.

"You have a visitor. Please go to the park to meet this person. Take your daughter with you." Although Selma was not yet four years old, I had been advised to take her with me any time I had an important meeting, so as to look less suspicious.

At the amusement park we walked around a lot and saw many people, but no one seemed to fit the description of the person we had been asked to meet. We sat down on a bench, and it was then that I noticed someone walking toward us. From his expression I realized he was the person we were looking for, and greeted him.

"Mrs Chipenda?"

"Yes."

"Do you speak French? English?" More through gestures than words, I managed to let him know that I understood a little of both languages but could not speak either one.

"I have been sent to meet you. You have the support of many people in organizations abroad, but could you tell me who is helping you with your plans here?"

When I mentioned the name of "the Boss", he said, "Oh yes, we know him. You are in good hands. I have come with the money you need to get out. Where can we meet again?"

"At church", I suggested, "at 9 o'clock tomorrow morning."

I went to church as usual. The morning service began and ended without my catching a glimpse of my visitor. I began to feel sick, and took the children right back to the hostel. At lunch I had the impression of eating rubber. I was unable to finish my meal. Evening came and still no sign of him. Then about 8 o'clock the doorbell rang. A couple of minutes later the maid came up to my room to announce his arrival. I met him at the top of the stairs. "Mrs Chipenda, I brought you a gift. Good luck." With that he handed me a package and disappeared. I took the present to my room. It was a box of chocolates.

Terror gripped me again. "I have been dealing with a secret agent. I'm doomed," I thought. The chocolates were passed around, and the box emptied. I went back to the room and threw it away. On Monday the rooms were cleaned, and Almerinda, the maid, collected my garbage bin. I had a nagging feeling, so on impulse I went and asked if I could have my bin back. I closed my door, pulled out the empty chocolate box, and stripped it. The money was at the bottom of the box, under layers of thick white paper.

I had never seen such a large pile of money, and it made me nervous. So I contacted "the Boss", and gave him the money, trusting that he would use it wisely. I felt liberated.

Later I related the events to my brother-in-law Daniel. He and his wife Guida had decided that they would have to leave with me, because Daniel had joined the political movement MPLA (*Movimento Popular de Libertacao de Angola*), which placed him under suspicion of the Portuguese authorities. But Guida was pregnant with their first child, and could not travel. We would have to wait for the child to be born. We were in a bind. As summer was drawing to an end, the number of tourists was thinning out; and as their numbers decreased, so did our chances of leaving the country unnoticed.

In September, I was given orders to prepare to leave. These orders were then withdrawn because the secret police were on the alert. Uncertainty continued to reign. What made the time of waiting bearable was the opportunity of meeting people and making friends from different parts of the world. The hostel attracted many interesting travellers because it was clean, inexpensive and safe. A friendly young woman from the USA stopped over for a short time on her way back home. As we chatted, it turned out that she had met my brother Job in Paris. When she left I sent along two dresses to Jose to let him know that we were still looking forward to coming.

Though I was lonely and depressed at times, I was sure that good angels were following and protecting us. They were present at the time I needed them. It has been my experience that God works through good people, very often through people with whom one has had no relations at all and whom one will never see again. I prayed a great deal during this time. I prayed that the Portuguese authorities might understand our suffering and allow our family to be reunited. I prayed for strength and perseverance. I also read much from the New Testament, especially the letters of Paul to the Philippians and Timothy. These served as an inspiration to me. In particular I took comfort from Paul's words to his colleagues in Christ about "running towards the goal". Although Paul and I had different directions to follow — his to run towards Christ, mine to run to the USA and to get there with the children safely — these words encouraged me to accept what was happening and to have faith.

By the time the definitive word to prepare to leave came, I had run out of money. I explained the situation to an expatriate couple, and they gave me some money. The husband, a medical doctor from the US who was studying Portuguese before being posted in Angola, wrote a prescription for a syrup that would help the children to sleep during our escape. Although foreign doctors were generally not authorized to prescribe medicine in Portugal, I went to the pharmacy and got the syrup. I also stopped at the grocery store to buy some apples, since the doctor had advised feeding the children with applesauce on the journey.

That Saturday I gathered a few articles of clothing for Gilbert and Selma, and put them in a small bag. A week before, I had packed a suitcase and taken it to "the Boss", who agreed to bring it on the day of the escape. In it were my clothes and a few mementoes — childhood and wedding photographs, a necklace and earrings given to me by a missionary on the day I left Angola and some beautiful fabrics that I had collected in Lisbon.

After I had organized our few things, I sat down to write a short note to the person in charge of the hostel. She had been very kind and helpful to me and the children, and I regretted that I could not say goodbye to her in person. In the note I explained the need for secrecy, and told the whole story of how I had tried to leave the country by legal means, but was now forced to escape. I asked that, should anything happen to me, my children be taken care of. Afraid that we might not make it, I asked that, if she heard we had been caught, she should try to get possession of the children and send them to their father where they would be safe.

On Sunday we went to church as usual. After lunch, I became very anxious. About four o'clock, I gave the note to the maid Almarinda, asking her to deliver it twenty-four hours later. We then took the tram to the park, and from there a taxi to an address that had been given to me. When we got out of the taxi, "the Boss" picked us up and we drove to another street, where my brother-in-law, his wife and their new baby, now just ten days old, were waiting. When a car suddenly stopped right alongside us, I felt a moment of panic, certain that it was the secret police. But the three passengers scarcely looked at us, and went on their way.

We drove until the early hours of the morning, finally arriving at a beach. When we got out of the car, I discovered that "the Boss" had not brought the suitcase I had left at his house. He had decided that it was too heavy for the trip. Deeply disappointed, I tried to ask him about it, but his only concern was getting us away. Every time I opened my mouth, he shouted, "Walk! Just walk!" Then he got back in his car and vanished. As I headed toward the waiting boat, I felt that I was leaving a part of myself that I would never find again.

A fisherman was waiting for us in his boat, and we had to wade in the water to reach it. Since the water level was high, the men took the children on their shoulders. Some of us, terrified by the water that now reached our shoulders, started screaming for help. Our voices were carried by the night wind, and the fisherman came closer.

I was soaking wet, but had nothing else to change into. We hid in the bottom of the boat. The fisherman was very kind to us. He made us tea and cooked very good meals, though Guida and I both became seasick and had a hard time holding down any food. With two young babies and both mothers sick, the men pitched in to help look after the children. Selma, who was four years old, did not understand the seriousness of what was happening, and was enjoying the adventure.

Our destination was the North African coast. We travelled for two-and-a-half days. When we approached Rabat, the fisherman put us in a canoe. He could not take the chance of coming too close to the harbour, since he might be arrested as a smuggler. The transfer occurred so quickly that we did not really have a chance to thank the fisherman. Soon he was out of sight.

None of us knew how to row. Daniel tried in vain to keep our spirits up and took the oars, but instead of moving us forward we kept moving backwards away from the harbour. It was the middle of the night, and all we could see were the lights of the harbour receding in the darkness. It became apparent that the canoe had a hole and was slowly filling up with water. Fortunately, a large Moroccan fishing boat was in the vicinity, and we started shouting for help. They approached us and threw us a line to pull the canoe up to the ship. We were helped onto the boat. The fishermen who had taken my son on board had to be coaxed to give him back to me. I had heard that Moroccan sailors stole babies and sold them to make money. I was terrified. Daniel and Guida realized what was going on, and helped me to grab the baby from him.

8. New York:
A Family Reunited

We were out of Portugal, finally, but the journey was not over yet. The Moroccan port authorities were at a loss as to what to do with us. It was night and the offices were closed. The children were cold, tired and hungry. A member of our group took off his jacket for them to lie on and I covered them with diapers. My mind was vague with exhaustion, and I wondered: "Why should I go through all of this?" How much easier and less dangerous it would have been if all of us — Jose, Selma and I — had left Angola together at the same time.

I was exhausted. I needed a quiet place, a corner of my own where I could take my mind to the state of Nirvana. I looked at my babies sleeping peacefully on the floor and I wished I were a child, young and innocent.

The next day we were taken by bus to Casablanca and lodged in two houses. A telegram was sent to Jose in New York. Our arrival was reported by Radio Morocco and by the Portuguese radio. Many people had worked to get us out of Portugal, and I would have loved to have been there to see their reaction at the news that we had made it.

Once again we waited while plans were made for us to join Jose in the United States. The general secretary of the United Church Board for World Ministries, the organization that funded Jose's studies and work in the USA, called John F. Kennedy, and appealed to him to issue travel documents so we could leave Morocco for the USA.

My nerves were on edge and I struggled to remain positive. All of my clothes were in the suitcase that had been left behind with "the Boss". I had to wash all of my clothes every night. Money soon arrived from Jose, and I was able to buy a skirt, blouse and a pair of sandals.

After two weeks of waiting, word came that we could leave. I gathered the few belongings we had, and my brother-in-law Daniel accompanied us to the airport. Daniel, his wife and their new baby stayed in Morocco until they were sent by MPLA to West Germany to continue planning and preparing for Angolan independence, which was still a distant dream. As I went through the departure gate, I wondered when and where we would all meet again.

It was a long plane ride. At first I was just glad to be on our way, but as we approached New York, I began to be very apprehensive. The idea of facing immigration officials in a foreign language filled me with dread. I had never travelled without a passport, and did not have much confidence in the piece of paper that was our travel document.

We landed late in the afternoon. As we followed the crowd of passengers to the immigration officials, I kept looking at the place where people were impatiently waiting for arriving friends and relatives. My eyes searched the crowd for Jose. Every time I saw a black person I waved, but got no response. We went through all the formalities and came out, but still no Jose.

I had a few moments of panic when I realized that no one was there to meet me and I was alone in a strange city. After waiting a short while, I decided to take matters into my own hands. Jose had sent me two addresses where I might find him: the Board of Missions at 475 Riverside Drive, and International House at Columbia University. Speaking no English at all, I hailed a taxi, got in with the children, and showed the driver the two addresses.

By now it was early evening, and the Board of Mission offices were closed, so the taxi driver took us to International House. There I went to the receptionist, only to be told that Jose was not in. Embarrassed, I went back out to try to explain to the taxi driver that I had no money. He just sat there and waited. Some people were passing by, and one gentleman stopped, enquired as to what the problem was, reached into his pocket and paid the cab driver. I thanked him, he went on his way, and I never saw him again. Only much later did I appreciate the depth of this gesture by one stranger to another.

Back at the reception desk, I told the woman who I was and she then explained that Jose had moved when he learned that his family would be coming. She thought he had gone to the airport to meet us, and wondered if our paths might have crossed. We were given a room to wait in, and I put the children to bed.

It was nearly ten p.m. when Jose finally found us. The telegram he had received had not specified our flight number or time of arrival. Our two-and-a-half-year ordeal was finally over. I felt as if a huge burden had been lifted from me. Our family was at last back together, and I would have someone with whom to share responsibility for the children.

Our family was finally reunited on September 21, 1962. Selma was nearly four, and Gilbert, the unborn baby Jose had left behind, was almost two.

Our first home in New York was a one-bedroom apartment in the Columbia University Teachers College. The apartment was unique, to say the least. The design was so awkward that I concluded that the architect must have been a man. The front door opened into the living room, but to get to the kitchen, toilet or bathroom one had to pass through the bedroom. The best thing about the apartment was that it was close to Riverside Drive, Riverside Church, International House, Morningside Drive, a park where the children could play and Harlem.

I found Harlem to be a fascinating area, a place of beauty and ugliness, good and bad, happy and unhappy people, rich and poor. A place with plenty of music and theatres, shops, well-stocked food stores, beautiful people, beauty salons and playgrounds. At the same time, Harlem was a place of great insecurity. Anything could happen to you at any time. You could be pickpocketed, robbed or intercepted at gunpoint. At first I got lost more than once, and had to stop and ask people for directions. Some people were very friendly and helpful, some would not stop to speak to me at all, some became aggressive.

It was already autumn when we arrived, and the weather was turning cold. This posed no problem though, because the story of "the woman who had escaped Portugal in a fishing boat" soon made its way around the North American missionary community and we were swamped with gifts: winter coats, clothes for the whole family, kitchen items, silverware, a huge old television set that never worked and an electric iron that also never worked.

One of the first things we did was go for medical examinations. Selma was fine; Gilbert had anaemia; and I had developed some sort of allergy that made my lips and face swell, and my body was covered in a red rash. The baby and I were put on medication, and all three of us had to get numerous vaccinations. I also went to see a gynaecologist. I was traumatized by the fact that my pregnancy had been used as a reason to separate the family. Jose and I did not want any more children, and after a two-and-a-half-year separation, we were not going to take any risks.

It did not take me long to adjust to a new way of life, since it was not my first trip out of Angola. The children were totally lost though, and cried much of the time. Everything was strange to them, including their own father. Selma had become close to her grandfather, and it was apparent that "father" was a vague concept to her. Once in Lisbon, someone had begun a prayer before the midday meal, "Our Father who art in heaven..." Selma immediately interrupted: "My father is not in heaven; he's in America."

I had assumed that she knew her father, but I was wrong. She missed the grandfather whose office she visited from time to time and whom she saw coming home each day. He was the one who took her on his lap and played with her. She also missed her friend Fernanda from Lisbon, and could not understand why we had left without saying good-bye. I had not talked to her about our departure before we left, because I had not wanted her to know just how frightened I was.

In Angola we were not accustomed to staying indoors. In fact, the only time anyone did so was when they were sick. So, in spite of the cold, I would take the children out to play in the nearby playground. It was well-equipped with swings, slides and sandboxes. The children liked the sandboxes best because that was where most of the other children played. I would sit on a nearby bench and watch. They were usually timid when approached by other children, but once a little boy of about Gilbert's age approached him and struck him in the face with a toy shovel.

Gilbert cried, then retaliated. But when the other child began to cry, Gilbert gave him a hug and kissed him. The two quickly became friends. At one point the child's mother joined me where I was sitting and we struck up a conversation. I knew very little English, but was able to catch a few words. When she discovered I had just arrived from Africa, her interest grew. She wanted to know where we came from in Africa, and which school the children were attending. Realizing that they were not yet enrolled, she volunteered to contact the director of the Riverside Church kindergarten and nursery school.

Jose came with me for the first appointment at the school because my English was not good enough, and I did not want to miss a single word of the conversation. Both Gilbert and Selma were accepted, but had to wait a term for some of the classes to open up. I was also offered a job as an assistant teacher in one of the nursery classes.

The first four months at the nursery were a little difficult because of my inability to communicate as I wanted. This did not seem to bother the children, who would come and cuddle against me whenever they were tired or unhappy. Gradually my English improved, and I was asked to assist the Sunday School teacher, which I did gladly for four years.

I grew to love New York. I enjoyed the freedom, the variety, the hustle and bustle of the city. There was always something to do or discover. The children and I were always glad when Jose could find time for us. Together we visited museums and parks, and roamed the streets. We discovered the cinemas, libraries and markets. We did not have many friends, but developed close ties with the few we had.

Shortly after our arrival, Jose took me to the Apollo Theatre with a colleague of his. While they conversed in English I took in the spectacle: the music, singing and dancing, the wonderful costumes, the energy of the entertainers and the elegance of the audience. I was elated, but self-consciously contained myself because I was terrified that someone would try to talk to me and I would not be able to reply.

When the Teachers College apartment was requisitioned, we moved uptown to a small apartment on Broadway. Shortly thereafter, we moved again to a basement apartment in a rather poor area of the city. The garbage cans stood not too far from our entrance, and since they were not emptied on a regular basis, the area was rat-infested. In spite of this, our neighbours kept piling their trash outside, and our complaints only seemed to make the situation worse. One day, disgusted by the whole situation, I took the children and went looking for a decent place to live. I enquired at every "for rent" notice I saw. We walked like crazy, and finally found a place I liked. The janitor, a short, stout and amiable man, must have noticed my desperation, and showed me an apartment on the fifth floor. I immediately made up my mind about it. Since I had no money for a down payment, I pleaded with him to hold the apartment long enough for me to bring my husband. As soon as Jose returned in the evening, I told him of our discovery and took him to see the place. Jose liked it too.

Our new apartment at 255 West 108th Street had one bedroom, a long corridor which became the children's room, a living/dining area, kitchen and bathroom. It was well lit and had windows all around — quite a step up from the basement to the fifth floor.

We struggled to make ends meet. Although Jose still had a scholarship, it was for a single student, and we were fortunate that the Board of Missions had agreed to pay our medical bills and rent. The little bit of money that I earned went to pay the children's school fees and supplement Jose's stipend. Jose's meagre savings were quickly used up, but he was able to do some youth work in a local congregation, which brought in some extra money. What we appreciated in the States was that we were always compensated for our work. If Jose was invited to preach on Sundays, or work with the youth, he was paid for his services. In Angola we were used to doing extra church work without being paid, which made it difficult for pastors' families to survive and often made us feel taken for granted.

My relationship with the Board of Missions was rather strained. I could not forget that they had been responsible for our staying behind in Angola, nor could I understand why, once the political situation in Angola had begun to change, they had not taken more active steps to reunite the family. At the same time, I could not ignore the contributions of individuals who had given a great deal of themselves to help us through. The Board of Missions never, to my knowledge, enquired about my needs; and I had the impression that they viewed me as a nuisance that they did not want to think about, though they felt obliged to be nice to me. We never asked for any more than they gave us, and got by with whatever means we could.

We had two unpleasant experiences with US Immigration. Some time after our arrival, we were notified that Mr Gilbert Chipenda, whom we were "harbouring", was an "illegal alien" and had 24 hours to leave the country. The whole family got dressed up and took the subway to the immigration office. We presented their letter and my papers, which indicated that the person they planned to deport was the three-year-old son of "legal aliens". The immigration official was embarrassed when he realized the mistake, and apologized for the inconvenience.

In 1964 the Board of Missions had arranged for a Ghanaian student to do a yearlong speaking tour of US university campuses. At the last minute the student was called back to Ghana by President Nkrumah, and Jose was asked to replace him. Everything went well until one day a letter arrived from the immigration office informing us that since Jose was in the US on a student visa, he was not supposed to be working. I panicked. Jose was always travelling, I did not know where to find him, and I immediately called the Board of Missions office, knowing that quick action was needed because the week's grace period given was coming to an end.

An agreement was reached between immigration and the Board of Missions. When I found out what that agreement was, I was outraged. It had been decided that Jose could continue with his work, but I would have to give up my job. I felt as if the ground had been swept from under my feet. I really enjoyed my job at Riverside Church. Even if my salary was not substantial, it was a steady source of income, and I was able to meet people and make a contribution. I remembered my father's advice to learn a skill, so that no matter what happened, I could always be self-reliant. I had never stopped sewing, and now I planned to take on more clients who paid for, and appreciated, my work. Later, the Board of Missions offered me the opportunity to enrol in a one-year secretarial course. I learned shorthand and typing, and got a degree.

While Jose was away on the tour, my time was divided between the secretarial classes and the children. I hardly had time for anything else, but one memory that stands out is of being invited to a Harry Belafonte concert by the Secretary for Africa of the United Church of Christ's Board of Missions. Belafonte had just returned from a tour in Africa, and I was thrilled by the prospect of seeing him in person. The concert was wonderful, and I was enticed by the chic of New York's night life.

Jose's travel documents expired during our stay in the US; and since it was impossible for us to obtain Portuguese passports, we were forced to file for refugee status. This made me feel suddenly displaced and empty, an intruder in a country not my own. I began to wonder constantly when we would be able to return to Angola. Later, a colleague of Jose's who had contacts at the Liberian consulate helped us to obtain Liberian passports. It felt strange suddenly to be a Liberian. I had never met any Liberians, and knew little about the country. But we were happy to have the documents.

9. From Geneva to Nairobi and Back

There was a small, fairly cohesive group of Angolans in the United States. We met for social events such as Christmas or weddings, and also gathered for meetings to analyze and discuss the political situation at home and share our experiences as Angolans living and studying in the United States. The one thing that could divide us, though, was politics.

At the time, there were two main independence parties in Angola: the *Movimento Popular de Libertacao de Angola* (MPLA), led by Agostinho Neto, and the *Fronte Nacional da Libertacao de Angola* (FNLA), led by Holden Roberto. The leaders of both parties had to operate from outside the country due to the oppressive situation inside. Their work was to mobilize resources and support from foreign governments for their cause.

Although MPLA and FNLA had the same goal — Angola's independence — they did not agree on much else and were constantly at odds. The MPLA was backed by the Soviet Union, and the FNLA was backed by the United States. The cold war was at its most frigid, and international political ideologies exacerbated the existing divisions between the two parties in Angola, which were primarily ethnic.

Since we had not aligned ourselves with either party and did not get involved in any political quarrels, our home became a neutral meeting ground. One year both Roberto and Neto were in the US at the same time. We knew them both, and invited them for a meal. Holden Roberto did not show up. For years during the struggle for independence, the two men refused to face one another, even though both were fighting for the same cause and both claimed to be defending the sovereign rights of "the people" and "their country".

A friend once took me to a meeting of liberation movement representatives, organized by a US support group. I could not see the point of the meeting. There was no presentation or real dialogue. The representatives seemed mainly concerned to have fun, and some eventually got drunk. All the while, their hosts of course remained sober. It was with some bitterness that I left that night. It seemed that when so much was at stake, we Africans typically forgot ourselves and the Americans always stayed in control. It was not the first time I had seen this happen, and the result was that Africans were continually being manipulated and taken advantage of, with truly horrible implications for their future.

In the mid-1960s the Angolan student association in the United States began to fall apart. A third political movement, the *Uniao Nacional de Independencia Total de Angola* (UNITA), led by Jonas Savimbi, was on the rise. UNITA was predominantly a movement of people from southern Angola — the Ovimbundu people — and many students in the US who were of Ovimbundu origin and had previously been associated with FNLA began joining the new party. This situation further fragmented an already divided community.

Jose finished his studies in 1966 and received an offer to work as the foreign student secretary for the World Student Christian Federation (WSCF) in Geneva, Switzerland. We were pleased finally to be finished with the student life and eager to begin a more permanent life in a new place.

The children were thrilled by the prospect of travelling by boat: an entire week on the *Queen Elizabeth I*. Meals were served in a central dining room, and Gilbert and Selma quickly befriended the waiter assigned to our table. The activities organized for the children on board during the day meant that there was rarely a dull moment. Unfortunately, the boat's continuous rocking got the better of Gilbert and me, and we were seasick for most of the journey, making meal times the most challenging part of the day!

In November 1966 we landed in London, from where we were supposed to apply for visas for Switzerland. London proved to be an interesting city. As in New York, there was a large black population. But although they spoke the same language in the two cities, the accent was so different that I understood scarcely a word. To add to the confusion, people drove on the other side of the street. I really had to gather all my wits to get around.

We were put up in a big old house. It was the beginning of winter, and London was covered in a thick, cold drizzle. The small coin-operated heater in our rooms barely kept us warm and quickly drove us towards bankruptcy. We applied for our visas, but the people at the Swiss consulate could not understand how Angolans had come to have Liberian passports, and we were denied entry into the country. Informed of the situation, the general secretary of the WSCF instructed us to proceed to Paris. We took a ferry across the English Channel. The crossing was a nightmare, and once again Gilbert and I suffered through the whole trip. I was feeling fed up and tired. It seemed that we would never reach our destination.

In France we stayed at the CIMADE (Comité Inter-Mouvement d'Aide aux Evacués) until our situation was sorted out. Eventually we were able to take the train to Geneva. The general secretary of the WSCF met us at the railroad station, and after a short time in a temporary residence, we moved to an apartment in La Gradelle.

We liked our new home. The apartment complex was not too far from the French border, and had everything we needed including a school, grocery store, pharmacy, doctor's offices and a community centre. Geneva was a small, quiet city with well-tended gardens and parks and an excellent public transportation system. Our neighbourhood was fairly international, and we met people from all over the world. People seemed less hurried and less aggressive than those in New York, and life was generally more relaxed and peaceful.

It did not take long for Jose to immerse himself in his new job and start travelling. The children picked up the new language and settled into school. It was a new chapter in our lives, and the whole family was happy to be in Geneva. I was struck by how neat everything was. When I first took the children to the park to play and saw the Swiss children there, I wondered if they ever got dirty. The mothers seemed to spend all their time saying: "Don't do this. Go here. Go there." I was fascinated by them, and they were equally curious to see us. At that time there were very few black people in Geneva. We were an attraction. Sometimes I enjoyed this feeling, but there were also times when we had to endure annoying discrimination.

I busied myself with equipping the apartment. Once again, I was challenged by the need to learn a new language. Even going to the bakery was an adventure. There was a variety of different types of bread and initially all I could do was guess, point, and smile. The baker must have thought I was mad. I started taking French and sewing classes at a school in downtown Geneva and learned French well enough to get by.

One thing that I missed was a beauty parlour that could do my hair properly. In Geneva, there was no beauty parlour for black people. I went once to a salon, but the woman said: "I'm sorry, we have no experience with black hair. I'm afraid we don't know what to do with it." I had no option but to go home and take care of my own hair.

Most of our friends and acquaintances were other foreigners working at the headquarters of such international organizations as the WSCF, World Council of Churches, YMCA and YWCA. They were from all over Europe, and I was fascinated by their cultures, their clothes, their styles.

A few Angolans dropped by occasionally to chat and catch up on news of home. Although we liked the life in Geneva and appreciated all of the opportunities that we had been given, we were as homesick as ever, and looked forward to the time when we could go home. Other African countries, such as Ghana, Kenya and Tanzania had achieved independence, and we anticipated the time when Angola would do the same. The war had been going on for six years, and there was no sign of a resolution. The international pressure being put on the Portuguese government only seemed to make it more stubborn. The fighting was bitter, with no end in sight. There was not much we could do except to continue to prepare ourselves by getting as much experience and training as we could so that when we went back home we could contribute to the development of our country.

* * *

On December 31, 1968, we left Geneva for Nairobi, Kenya. Jose and two other people had been appointed to open two Africa regional offices for the WSCF, one in Nairobi, the other in Cameroon. Arriving in Nairobi on New Year's Day, we were met by one of Jose's colleagues and his fiancee as well as the general secretary of the All Africa Conference of Churches (AACC). It was a beautiful crisp morning. The sky was blue with a few white clouds scattered here and there. The fresh morning air was such a delight that we soon forgot the heavy winter and snow left behind. As we walked towards the immigration office at the Jomo Kenyatta airport, Selma stopped for a second, looked around with some astonishment and curiosity. "Are we in Africa?", she asked. Neither she nor Gilbert had any memories of Africa, only the images conveyed in Switzerland, and their main question was where the animals were.

In fact, apart from the weather, the Jomo Kenyatta airport at that time was quite reminiscent of the airport we had just left in Geneva: small, compact, clean and very accessible to the city. Nairobi itself seemed to have many similarities to Geneva, small but very neat and clean, not crowded as it is today. In the downtown area there were few cars and lots of parking spaces. The only large buildings were the Hilton Hotel, the Kenyatta International Conference Centre, and a few banks. The telephone, water and electrical systems worked reasonably well. Gardens and public places were well taken care of. Apart from the slums, the ugly side of many cities in Africa, Nairobi was a colourful city with plants, trees and a profusion of flowers of all kinds and colours.

We were happy to be in an African country, particularly for the sake of the children. Although Jose and I had no idea of when Angola would become independent, we felt that exposing Selma and Gilbert to the experience of living in an African country could be a good introduction to the time when our country would be freed and we would return. We were conscious that Kenya was not our country and that we were visitors, people in transit, and we concentrated our efforts on what had brought us there, to learn from our stay.

I was happy not to be part of a minority, as we had been in Europe. The Swiss people we had encountered in Geneva at that time had not been very exposed to black people, in part perhaps because it was a country that had no colonies in Africa. While our experience was not negative in every respect, one unpleasant incident did remain in my memory as typical of this sense of exclusion. I had taken the children to town for shopping, and as we entered one store we were the focus of great attention. We were called *les nègres*, the blacks. We moved around the shop at ease, but the woman at the cashier's counter could not resist: she touched my son's arm with her hand as though wanting to know if it was dirty or not. I simply could not understand her mind at all. I found it absurd, and lamented that people could be so ignorant about others. On the other hand, in Nairobi, I was once called a refugee by an angry Kenyan woman at the workshop where I was training people in dressmaking. Knowing that my family and I had not come to Kenya as refugees, I was able to ignore the sting of her remark as coming from someone who had problems of her own. Several years later, during our second stay in Geneva in 1974, things had changed noticeably. *Les nègres* were so many, that the Swiss and other Europeans seemed to have got past the novelty; and there were marriages between the Swiss and *les nègres*.

The house we were to occupy in Nairobi was not ready, so we were taken to the AACC Training Centre where two rooms had been reserved. Right away, Jose got busy setting up an office. The children were enrolled at Kilimani primary school. It was some distance from the centre, so I spent much of my time during the first few weeks escorting them to and from school.

Before we left the AACC training centre to move to our new house I met a young Kenyan woman who visited the centre a couple of times. Thanks to her radiant smile and approachable personality we soon became acquainted. We were the first Angolans she had ever met so she wanted to know more about us and our coming to Kenya. It had not occurred to me to look for a job, but after I told her I was a seamstress and teacher she asked me if I would like to work and she put me in contact with the general secretary of the YWCA. An appointment was made and soon after we met with a small group of young women to discuss the possibility of beginning a training programme in dressmaking and design. At the time there were not many Kenyan women engaged in this field.

I visited the YWCA a few times to locate a vacant room where the classes could be held. Next I ordered tables to be made and contacted local business people for donations. We obtained supplies and twelve new sewing machines on condition that we promoted our sponsors. The project started with twelve women, all from different cultural and social backgrounds. Some of them could not read or write and to mark the dimensions they had to fold the tape measure and apply it to the pattern or fabric. Since some students spoke little or no English at all and I spoke no Swahili, communication was sometimes complicated, but I had the time of my life!

Most of the women had families and were struggling simply to survive. One member of the group told me she dreamed of having twelve children, although she was already facing enormous problems trying to bring up six children without the assistance of a husband. I wondered how she could possibly manage if her dream did come true.

Because the pedal machines at work could only do straight stitching, it was very tedious to make a properly finished garment. In order to introduce the students to different kinds of sewing machines and show them how to zig-zag and make buttonholes, one day I brought my electric sewing machine from home to class. The women watched with fascination, but only two of the women were willing to try it themselves. When I asked why they hesitated, one of the came to me very quietly and said, "We are afraid that handling an electric machine might make us infertile."

As time went by and the students learned to love working with the machines, we spent many wonderful moments together. With them I learned tolerance and understanding, and I learned to admit my limits. They taught me the futility of knowledge without the ability to communicate and exchange, and the importance of helping each other to achieve our goals.

With Jose spending more and more time travelling throughout Africa to meet with university students, I saw the need to learn to drive. Going to work using public transportation was a great challenge. Buses, which ran irregularly, were considered full only when it was impossible to hang from the last step; and during the rush hours people would literally pile on top of each other. In the hot season it was intolerable.

It was common knowledge that the best way to pass the driving test was to bribe the examiner. When I failed the test the first time, I immediately booked for the second and took a few more lessons for practice. One day the instructor came to our house, apparently downcast. Before taking me for the lesson he explained that he had just received word from the village that his mother was very ill, and that he needed to go and see her before it was too late. He asked me for a loan of one hundred Kenya shillings until the next payday. I did not know whether or not to believe him. It was rare, even unthinkable for a man to approach a woman, especially one from a different cultural background, for money. Nor was the loan negligible: one hundred Kenya shillings would have paid for one week's worth of groceries. At the same time, I wondered, "What if the story is true and I refuse to help?" I lent him the money. Shortly thereafter, I passed the second test and he took charge of getting me the driving licence. After that I never saw him — or the hundred shillings — again.

The assassination of Tom Mboya, one of the ministers in President Jomo Kenyatta's government and the most powerful opposition leader in Kenya at that time, triggered a wave of tribal conflict in the country. Kenyatta was Kikuyu, Mboya a Luo. Even though things were going very well with my group of women at work, I was told by management that henceforth I could train only Kikuyu women. I could not see the logic in that, especially since, as a foreigner, I could not distinguish between Kikuyus and non-Kikuyus. What mattered to me was that they were all Kenyan. The idea of depriving someone from learning just because she was different revolted me, and I ended up leaving the YWCA.

Two months after my resignation, I was contacted by Maridadi, a fabric printing project based in Pumwani, one of the slums of Nairobi. The aim of the project was to involve disadvantaged women in revenue-generating activities and to restore their human dignity. I was struck by the similarities between the situation of women in Pumwani and those in Angola. I watched the constant movement of women and children carrying buckets of water on their heads. They encountered so many obstacles that most of the water, it seemed to me, was spilled as they walked. Nor could I ignore the curses, quarrels and sometimes fights caused by the anxiety and despair of standing in a long line for hours before getting to the water fountain. It was impossible not to see the market women sitting all day under the sun alongside the roads covered with plastic sheets selling small heaps of vegetables and fruit, often next to a pile of rotten garbage and stinking toilets. What a life!

In Pumwani I was asked to start up a sewing department and provide training for women. Again, a work space had to be located, painted and furnished. About a hundred women were involved in the project. Some did the printing, others made place mats, neckties, cushion covers, aprons and bags. In my department we made very simple but comfortable dresses and summer shirts. At Maridadi I met a Finnish textile designer who had come to Nairobi to work as a volunteer. Together we met with Kenyan textile designers and developed new patterns for the project. Maridadi was a unique place in Nairobi in that it attracted business people, nationals and non-nationals, tourists and the diplomatic corps. All these people flocked in during visiting and business hours.

Just before I started my second year in the sewing department, Jose got a call from the World Council of Churches in Geneva and was offered a new position. The family talked about it, and we decided to go. While Jose prepared his departure from the WSCF, I began preparing for the second move that year, since we had just moved into a new house in Nairobi. The prospect of going to Geneva was not bad, but I was getting tired of the constant packing and unpacking. Also, the work at Maridadi was becoming the realization of a dream. I would very much have liked to continue exploring printing techniques and to experiment with colours and textile design. I dreamed of starting a similar project in Angola after independence.

* * *

We left Nairobi on December 31, 1973. Jose joined the World Council of Churches (WCC) as director of the Programme to Combat Racism (PCR). The work involved extensive travelling and networking in Africa, Europe, the Americas, the British Isles and Asia. South Africa and its system of apartheid was making headlines. Along with Angola, Namibia, Mozambique and Zimbabwe (then Rhodesia) were fighting for independence. Other Portuguese colonies such as the Cape Verde Islands, Guinea Bissau and Sao Tome were in turmoil. Leaders of the political movements of many of these countries travelled to Europe to find allies. Some met Jose at work, others came to our house to visit.

Looking back, I cannot help thinking that while it was easy to condemn colonialism, we were not always clear enough about what political system would replace it and how it would work. Too often political decisions seemed to be based on where a group could get financial help and weapons to fight the oppressor. There were often several competing independence movements — three in the case of Angola — but it sometimes seemed that it was not different convictions but the quest for personal political power that acted as the major dividing force. I could not understand why leaders of political movements from the same country, speaking about the same people, fighting for the same cause, could not look each other straight in the eye. Even more painful now is to see weapons once used to eliminate the oppressor, the colonial masters, turned on their own people, and countries being thrown into deeper misery and poverty.

To my surprise our neighbourhood in Geneva, La Gradelle, had not changed much, and to a great extent we picked up where we left off. Selma and Gilbert quickly adapted to the move and started attending the International School of Geneva. After school and during the summer holidays they found jobs. Selma baby-sat and during the summer worked for the YWCA and, later, the WCC. Gilbert eventually found a job caddying at the golf course.

As is the case in many other Christian organizations, the wives of expatriate staff members, many of whom were highly qualified and had left jobs of their own to accompany their husbands, were largely ignored and had little if any chance of finding employment. To keep busy, I first renewed my membership with the WCC wives' group, of which I was invited to be president in 1975. The group, founded by women to cater to their common interests and concerns, organized a variety of cultural, artistic and educational activities according to the interests of the members. For someone interested in arts and crafts, as I was, Geneva was in many ways an ideal place to live. I took a course a number of classes in textile printing and serigraphy, and enrolled in a correspondence course in interior design. I had little acquaintance with the latter when I signed up for the pro-gramme, but fortunately I met an architect, who became my mentor, and I did well in the course.

Although I was doing some sewing for individual clients, I wanted to have a steady salary and some savings of my own. After looking for employment for some time, I applied in person and was hired for a position listed in the local paper. My employer had a small studio and two seamstresses working for him. One of them, for one reason or another, was not at all pleased by my presence. She was asked to introduce me to the work, but she did not. The second, more quiet and reserved but very perceptive, shared her work with me to keep me busy. On the third day I took the fashion sketches I did in school in New York to show them to my employer, and he liked some of them. But the first woman also looked at them and said dismissively, "I did the same in school." Again, I sat the whole morning with nothing to do. On the fourth day I stayed at home and called in to announce my resignation. My own customers continued to come and I was happy.

During the times when Jose was able to take some days off work, we visited a number of places in Europe — Rome, Venice, Paris, the Netherlands, West Germany — as well as travelling to different regions of Switzerland to explore the beautiful sites of the country. Since La Gradelle was near the border, we often ventured into neighbouring France. It was wonderful to be and do things together as a family, and we tried to make the best of those times.

In 1975 Angola finally became an independent country, and I was haunted by an urgent desire to take the children home to visit Jose's and my families. I had told them so much about Angola, the country of their birth. I had talked about my brother Julio, and my nephews, their uncles. Now I wanted everything to be real for Selma and Gilbert. I wrote to Julio to ask him to obtain travel documents for us, and he was thrilled with the idea. At first he seemed very optimistic that there would be no problems, but he soon realized that the Ministry of Immigration and Defense was not being responsive to our request; and the planned trip had to be cancelled. Selma and Gilbert were sent instead to Lisbon to learn Portuguese. It had been Selma's first language and she had not forgotten it completely, but Gilbert's spoken Portuguese was limited to the words "mama" and "papa". They both picked it up quite easily.

Before Selma and Gilbert went to college in the US, Jose and I contemplated the possibility of returning home for good. The thought was shared with them but Gilbert in particular was not happy about it. "Why now?", he asked. "Why not wait to see us through college?" In 1976 Selma finished high school and left; two years later Gilbert followed. With Jose gone much of the time on travel connected with his work, the house had become an empty cage. I always looked forward to the summer holidays when Selma and Gilbert came home.

The summer of 1980 was the last summer together for the four of us. Jose and I had made the decision to return to Angola for good. We felt it was time to contribute to the development of our own country. Selma and Gilbert were assured of their financial and spiritual assistance in college. It was time to go our own ways. Yet soon after independence, Angola had plunged into civil war, and I wondered in silence when we would see our children again. When they left to go back to the USA that summer, I felt something tear within me.

10. Lobito: Home Again

Jose had one more trip to make before we finally left Geneva. The responsibility of packing fell on me once again. Up and down to the basement I went, putting things together and doing the inventory before the moving company arrived. When Jose returned, there was nothing left in the flat except the suitcases we would travel with. I was dead tired and furious: "Why me all the time?", I asked. When the day arrived to take the train to Paris, where we were to stop en route to Angola, any desire to make myself presentable had gone. To make it worse, my hair refused to obey the comb. I travelled with a head scarf and avoided looking at my hands.

The trip to Angola was an ordeal. We were scheduled to fly on Alitalia but upon arriving in Rome we learned that the airline had suspended operations with Angola, so we had to be rerouted via Lisbon. The trip from Lisbon to Angola was another nightmare. The plane was fully booked, and since we did not have seats we had to spend a night in Lisbon. Early in the morning we left the hotel for the airport, which was once again chaotic with people, shopping bags and luggage left behind by Angolans who had travelled to Portugal for medical treatment, shopping or various other reasons. The civil war had plunged the country into serious problems, and anyone who could get away did so, either temporarily or permanently.

We checked in, paid for our excess luggage and boarded. We were on the way to a troubled country to start a new life. "Had we really made the right decision?" was the question that constantly came to my mind, though on balance I was convinced it was the right time to be back home close to events. When we arrived in Luanda, we found out that there were no connections to Benguela, a mere 35-minute flight away. Two hectic days were spent in Luanda looking for ways and means to travel to our final destination. On the morning of the third day we were taken to the airport very early. The day progressed with little sign of any hope of reaching our final destination. We were hungry and thirsty, but there were no drinks or food to be found. The airport was full of trash to the extent that you had to watch where you stepped. The toilets did not flush and were filthy and smelly. I felt sorry for the women, some with babies on their backs, who were trying in vain to do some cleaning when the public so evidently did not care. I heard someone shouting: "Down with the bourgeoisie! This is an independent country! We are a free people!", while at the same time throwing banana peels on the floor.

When the announcement that it was time to board for Benguela finally came everyone surged forward, anxious to get onto the plane. We managed to arrive in Benguela safely, but no one had come to meet us, because communication between Luanda and the provinces had not been possible. Jose's brother Duarte, who lived in Lobito, a city 25 to 30 minutes' drive from Benguela airport, was shocked when a car suddenly pulled up in front of his house and there we were! His eyes were filled with tears. We hugged him and his wife and children. Emotions were high. "Why have you come to this troubled country? Why didn't you remain in Geneva?", they wanted to know. "The situation here is very bad, and the name Chipenda is unpleasant to many," Duarte explained. "Fortunately I have some friends and good colleagues in the bank where I work; otherwise, I would be dead or in prison by now."

Jose's brother Daniel was a politician who had apparently become *persona non grata* to the political movement. He had fought bravely against colonialism but was now, after independence, viewed with suspicion in a country where democracy had never existed and citizens were judged according to their political affiliations. The situation had worsened when the Portuguese rulers and other Western foreigners moved out of Angola in panic and were replaced by Cubans and those from the Soviet bloc. The civil war began with the leaders of the three movements competing with each other for power and proselytes. One movement took power, one went into the bush, and the third went into exile. Daniel went into exile with the third movement, and for many years stayed out of Angola wondering when he could return.

Duarte was not at all politically involved. His life centred on his family, job, soccer team, church and the friends he cultivated throughout his life. A devoted and generous servant of others, he had difficulty keeping his own car in good repair because he was always ready to lend it to almost anyone. Yet because their brother Daniel was involved in politics, Duarte and the rest of the Chipendas, although respected and admired for their work, were always viewed with suspicion. My sister-in-law once remarked: "This name Chipenda is really something. Sometimes I wish I could change it to another."

After dinner Duarte took us to our own house, which he had acquired for us from a Portuguese family who had decided to leave Angola. Duarte had kept it patiently during our stay in Geneva, awaiting our arrival. We liked the house inside and out. I especially cherished the garden and the profusion of plants around it. The Portuguese family had left it half furnished, so when our belongings arrived from Geneva, we had everything we could have wished for, including a car. Indeed, while unpacking the boxes, we realized we had more than we needed.

Lobito had changed dramatically since Jose and I had last seen it. There was garbage everywhere. Food, electricity, water and cooking gas were in seriously short supply. The rate of infant and adult mortality was high, and people lined up in the cemeteries to bury the dead. Yet we were home. We had decided to go home to work with people in any way we could under the circumstances, to try to make a difference. Despite everything, we were happy to be home and to have our own house, where we could relax after a day of work and worries.

It took almost no time to make new aquaintances and friends. After putting our belongings in order, we began finding ways and means of setting up a Centre of Studies of Theology and Culture in 1981. The centre would offer theological, cultural and training programmes for women and youth, as well as activities for children. Sunday school teacher training programmes, refresher courses for church leaders and pastors, and seminars and workshops for clergy and lay persons were developed for those working at the provincial and national levels. We succeeded in getting running water for the centre, and began furnishing it with some of our own belongings — chairs, sofas, tables and the like. What we were doing quickly became known to the public, as well as to politicians, members of the Party and representatives of the government of the province of Benguela and of the central government in the capital. Some of them did not hesitate to send their wives and children to participate in the programmes offered at the centre. Meetings and activities of common concern were shared with Catholic fathers and sisters.

The centre provided training to those who needed to be trained, regardless of their religion, race, colour or social and political affiliation. This was something quite different from what I had experienced when I was growing up in Angola, when the usual practice was for the Catholics to take care of their converts in their missions and schools and for the Protestants to do so in theirs.

Finding food and other basic commodities continued to be a struggle in Lobito, as elsewhere in the country. One day, on the way to work, I saw a pickup truck full of oranges, tangerines, pears and apples being unloaded in front of a shop. Immediately a woman came up to me and asked what I wanted.

"I came to buy what you have here," I replied.

"Well, you have to see the director first." I walked up the staircase and found a secretary's office. She called her boss, and I was given permission to see him. He was an old cordial and polite Portuguese man, a remnant of colonial times who had decided to remain in Angola. After greeting him I explained the reason for my visit. On a piece of paper he wrote down something, and with that note, I did the shopping.

When I went to the cashier the same woman intercepted me again, this time more aggressively. "So, you are a Chipenda? Are you a sister of Chipenda, the politician?"

"I am his sister-in-law, yes."

"Oh. This shop is only for the cooperants, the members of the Party and the militants of the government."

One Sunday in church I met an elderly man who had known me as a little girl in primary school. We spoke briefly; then he fixed his eyes on me as if he had never seen me before. "I am so glad you and your husband have come back," he said. "We need you to help us to pull the church together. We are getting old. We need younger people. We sent our sons to be educated abroad, but now they have come back to kill us." Other people looked back to the time when the political movements were outside the country fighting for independence. "There was no distinction between people of the south, the north, the west, the east, in the prisons and deportation camps we were sent to by the colonial rulers," they said. "We were one people. Now that the political movements have come to the country, we are divided."

Such was the political uncertainty in the country that no one could ever predict what might possibly occur on any given day or night. One day I was awakened when our doorbell rang at five o'clock in the morning. When I looked out the window and saw five armed men in uniforms, I ran to wake up Jose. "Jose, we have visitors. Army people." He got up, dressed quickly and went downstairs. I followed him, standing at the main door. I saw Jose talking to them, then opening the door gate. "Who are you and what brought you here?", he asked.

"We came to inspect the house," said the soldiers.

They searched the house thoroughly, opening drawers, closets, suitcases and leaving the kitchen upside down. Jose was calm but I was nervous, then began to argue and finally ran downstairs to make a phone call to a member of the Party to inform them about what was happening. But the telephone lines were cut and the whole of Lobito had no communication.

Back upstairs, the search continued. "Why are you doing this?", I asked.

"Orders received," one of them replied.

"Orders from whom?"

"From the authorities." One soldier looked at me with a sweet but strange smile. "Why are you nervous?", he asked.

"Because this never happened to us in the colonial days," I retorted, disgusted and hurt.

They finally left the house at 7 a.m. Later we learned from neighbours that the army had surrounded some areas of Lobito and conducted a house-to-house search. Any young men who were found were taken and sent immediately to the battle front. Many were caught that morning. We saw some in trucks, others chained, waiting for transportation. They looked sad and despairing. To many it was tantamount to a death sentence. Many were never seen again; of those who came back many were deformed. Later we would see soldiers coming to be buried at home, as well as truckloads of wounded soldiers being brought to the hospitals. Many parents travelled long distances trying to locate their loved ones. War is an ugly business, and the wounds are never fully healed.

A couple of months later, when another group of soldiers came to our house, Jose was out of the country, so I had a logical and a legal defense. They were three armed men; I was a woman alone and unarmed. They asked if we had a son or any other young man living with us, and I simply replied, "No." No son nor any other young man, thank God. They stood still and I did the same, looking at them until they moved away quietly. The heartbreak of war touches all the citizens of a country, including the soldiers. Many were taken at the age of 15 — some from their beds, others on their way to school. Some boys left for school in the morning and never arrived home at the end of the day. Weeks and months would go by. All around the country I saw desperate mothers travelling in search of their sons. The long and painful war continues. The twenty years since independence have been lost without any gains. There has been time only for the destruction of human lives and property, and the country is upside down.

The country we had come home to was bleeding. The programmes at the Centre of Studies of Theology and Culture were beginning to have an impact, and we thanked God for that. But the agony of the war and its consequences, the despair that could be read in people's faces, the hopelessness confronting the youth were heavy burdens to cope with. It was hard to hear a young man of school age say: "Why plan for the future? I am going to be picked up by the army anyway." Meanwhile, I was thinking of my own children in college abroad, wondering if they could ever return to Angola and looking for an opportunity to visit them.

11. Luanda: Learning and Teaching

In my youth I often heard testimonies from church leaders arriving at or being sent to a new post. It was common for them to say, "The Lord has sent me here" or "I am going where the Lord is sending me". Very often I found myself wondering if it was really the Lord or someone claiming to speak on his behalf.

We had put a great deal of effort into starting the programme for the Centre of Studies of Theology and Culture. There was tremendous participation from young and old, women and men. Then, just as the centre was beginning to get into full swing, the leaders of the Angolan churches appointed Jose to the position of general secretary of the Angolan Christian Council of Churches. This meant moving to Luanda and leaving the centre without a replacement in view.

Jose had to leave almost immediately, but I stayed on in Lobito until someone could be found to continue the training programme. Once in the capital, he discovered that the Council had not reserved a house for the general secretary and his family. For a while he occupied a small room in an apartment rented by a Dutch couple also employed by the organization. He moved out when the couple no longer welcomed him; and an Angolan employee of the Council put him in a guest house used by those coming from the provinces who had no other place to stay.

When the time came for me to join Jose in Luanda, the packing process fell on me once again. In Lobito there were no moving companies. I did everything, walking up and down with heavy boxes, sorting out what to take to Luanda and what to leave behind. The women's project was left with one of my students, a very responsible young woman. Jose came to find a tenant for our house and deal with other pending family matters. Finally everything was finished, and we travelled together to Luanda.

I did not remember having seen piles and piles of garbage everywhere on my previous visits to Luanda. Now, as we were driven to our new home I began to wonder where I was being taken. The house where Jose was staying was not one we could consider our home. It belonged to the Christian

Council, and continued to be used as a guest house after we moved in. There were three bedrooms, one bath and toilet upstairs, a common living and dining room, a shower, pantry, kitchen and laundry space downstairs, but no running water. The water had to be fetched from outside early in the morning before the pressure had gone. We filled every possible container — the bathtub, wash basins, several buckets and whatever bottles we had. The neighbourhood had been a good one in colonial days, but the war had changed everything. Along with the water, the garbage system and electricity had disappeared with the colonialists. The house hosted an army of cockroaches, and rats ran in and out constantly. The same fate had befallen people almost everywhere in Luanda. On top of all of these problems, the area was very sandy and dusty, and the more you cleaned the house the dirtier it looked.

Things Jose had ordered from abroad were sitting in the living room still covered in plastic because he did not know how long we would stay in this place. We found two guests in the house and more kept coming. I cooked, cleaned and fetched water from outside. Laundry day was one of the worst days of my life. The guests, on the other hand, seemed happy to have somebody to do this for them. It was becoming too much for me. Carrying water to the house and filling the containers was my daily song. I became ill, and Jose feared for my health as I did for his. I had hurried to Luanda to join him, and now we were suffering together.

Jose began looking for and eventually found another house, which had running water, electricity and a telephone. It was close to the main hospital and not far from the Council offices. After the family occupying it finally moved out I spent three days cleaning the walls and the floors. Again, there were cockroaches everywhere. We bought some appliances, painted the walls, scraped the kitchen floor which was covered with a thick layer of cooking oil. By the time I was finished, the place looked decent and comfortable.

For two years Jose dedicated himself to the work of the organization. A relief programme was well under way and the response from the donor agencies was great. Not only food, clothing and medicine were sent, but also vehicles to transport the goods to the needy in different areas of the country. The drivers, to whom I pay my respect, risked their lives to cover long distances and bring hope and life to those they were able to reach. The director of the Christian Council's women's desk asked me to implement a women's training programme in Luanda along the lines of the one in Lobito. I met with a group of women, listened to their needs, then made a list of materials needed. Together, the director and I put together a proposal for submission to foreign donors. We received everything we needed: twenty pedal sewing machines, five electric sewing machines, lots of fabrics, boxes and boxes of sewing notions, buttons, thread of all colours, hand and machine needles, knitting needles, wool and a vehicle to transport women to the Centre. We worked outdoors under the shade provided by a zinc roof while a new training centre financed by Norwegian Church Aid was under construction. Seminars and workshops for youth, women and church leaders were organized.

In August 1987, Jose was invited to attend the All Africa Conference of Churches' general assembly in Lomé, Togo. The search for a new general secretary for this continental ecumenical organization was underway, and although Jose had not put forward his candidacy, he was chosen to lead the AACC. Suddenly he found himself caught between two organizations, one national and the other continental. Not being able to move to Nairobi as soon as expected, Jose commuted between Angola and Kenya for about eight months, completing two years of a four-year mandate with the Angolan churches.

Was it a call from God? It is hard to tell. But let me not question whether it was or not. In any case, I had to do the packing alone again. I stayed behind in Luanda for more than six months. The director of the women's desk asked if I would help her to find a replacement staff person for the women's training programme. I thought of another student of mine in Lobito as a possibility. She was contacted and we worked together for two months so that she could become acquainted with the work and students.

Once again I was being forced to leave an activity I enjoyed. No longer would I be able to learn from the students' experiences, some of which were incredible. No longer would I be able to teach them some of the skills I had learned and which they were so eager to share.

12. Nairobi: Looking Ahead in Hope

Jose returned from Nairobi to hand over to his successor his responsibilities at the Angolan Christian Council. On March 28, 1988, the two of us left Angola for a new home. Nairobi was not an unknown destination, nor was the house in which we were going to live, since we had visited the former general secretary of the AACC there several times. It is a good and comfortable house in one of the best locations of the city. The garden is spacious with well-tended plants of different kinds. Behind the house I planted vegetables: sweet corn, potatoes, beans, lettuce, tomatoes and lemon grass, which I serve with pride to our guests. I had little to do inside except make new curtains and change the colour of the kitchen walls and closets.

A few weeks after our arrival in Nairobi, I woke up with a sharp pain at the back of my neck. I could not sleep any more; and at one o'clock in the morning Jose took me to the emergency room where the X-rays showed a small dislocation of the bone in my spinal column. Later that same morning another doctor saw me. The treatment prescribed was simple: no tablets, no injection — just a small twist of the neck to the left and right. I screamed of course, but it took care of the pain. The doctor suggested that the dislocation was caused by lifting heavy boxes.

The first years in Nairobi were not good ones. After leaving rewarding jobs in Lobito and in Luanda, I found myself in a foreign country often alone because of the seemingly endless travels of my husband. Sometimes I felt stupid, forgotten, put in a corner against the wall. At other times I heard voices talking to me. "Move, woman! Find your own way out. Fight it alone! Go, go ahead!" I began to question my own existence. I wondered whether it was the will of God or human will that put me through all these ordeals. Why was it not possible for me to have the pleasure of a steady career without all these interruptions? Was it God's will that I should always have to stand up alone, find my own way out? Did my husband actually realize what I was going through, or was he too preoccupied with the organization, the well-being of staff, their salaries, the education of their children and their work performance? How many married men enquire about the well-being of their wives when they come home for lunch or return at the end of the working day, before relating their own worries, successes and defeats, and those of the staff?

Yes, you try to go ahead, but there are so many road-blocks on the way. How many times I came to think the world we live in is not a world of the studied, the intelligent, the world of intellectuals, of the capable. No, it is the world of the lucky ones: that counts so much more.

Of course I was always grateful on the few occasions that I was assigned to travel with Jose. It was an opportunity to meet people — a chance to interact with them and to participate in meetings; to listen to people's concerns about their countries and the organizations they work with, the economic and political problems of the world, and, in particular, the problems of Africa; to come to know other African countries and some of their heads of states; in short, to learn from others and to get away from the house. I looked forward to these trips like a child waiting for a sweet.

Jose and I travelled home before the end of 1988, stopping in Harare, Zimbabwe, where he met with a Norwegian church delegation. At dinner I joined three of them and a Zimbabwean woman who was deputy general secretary of the Christian Council there. I was not noticed until she introduced me as the wife of the general secretary of the All Africa Conference of Churches. Suddenly, they looked at me with new interest. "How do you feel being the wife of a general secretary of such a big and important organization?", they asked.

"I was his wife before he became General Secretary of AACC", was my immediate reply.

In the AACC and other ecumenical circles I discovered that meetings often opened with personal introductions, presumably so that the participants could get to know each other better. Some people took the opportunity to list all the titles they had earned, and all the places and countries they had visited and organizations they had worked for. Others with as many titles were more modest when introducing themselves. All my life I had been known as the daughter of my parents or the wife of the General Secretary; and at times I found it hard to say who I was, so I would simply gave my name and my country of birth. The personality of my parents is the banner I have carried throughout.

During this period of self-questioning I became involved in a project that allowed me to test and exercise my skills and talents in a new way. For seventeen years the All Africa Conference of Churches could be identified by a gigantic unfinished building which could be seen from the side of a busy road near downtown Nairobi. Construction on this conference centre had begun years earlier, but had been halted because of a lack of funds. The building was circular, reflecting the shape of an African hut, with a majestic Coptic cross on the roof. The architecture was beautiful, but as the years went by the unfinished building became the focus of a lot of attention. After much consultation, it was decided to finish the building. A building committee composed of architects, business and finance people, church leaders and lay people was formed. I received a letter of invitation from the AACC administrative office, asking me to be one of two people assigned to monitor the construction project. When I accepted, my colleague turned to me and said, "Eva, now it is your time to shine."

Although I was involved in all aspects of the project, the chapel, landscaping, main entrance and interior design of the building were my principal responsibilities. After a good deal of thought, it occurred to me that we could use African religious symbols for this continental Christian organization which represents more than 140 churches and councils in Africa. Although there are stylistic differences, the meaning of the symbols is no different from those used in Western Christianity.

I worked closely with a Ugandan sculptor living in Kenya to design and execute a number of large carved wooden panels which stand majestically in the middle of the main entrance hall. Standing in front of them one can see God's perfect creation of man and woman, as well as the outworking of this creation — life, sin, repentance, death and resurrection represented in the form of a cross, the symbol that all Christians carry, in so many different ways, a symbol which binds Christians and non-Christians everywhere in a common destiny and brings together Christians and member churches of this important continental organization. The artist, his assistants and I worked very hard towards the realization of this dream. We looked forward to the completion date, and on inauguration day we were extremely tired but happy for the legacy we had helped create.

* * *

What next? Some questions in this book may not find an answer. When I look back at the positive and negative aspects of my life as a "visitor", I can see that I grew to be a woman, a balanced person. Writing this book has helped to put me at peace with myself. I am hopeful, too, that peace will come to Angola. With the help of the outside world, efforts are being made to shape up the social and economic and political situation, above all bringing the political factions together and to common sense. There is hope!